Andrew Stevenson is a practising solicitor advocate at Waddell and Mackintosh, Troon. He first appeared in the small claims court in 1989, gave a seminar for the Royal Faculty of Procurators in Glasgow when new Summary Cause and Small Claims rules were introduced in 2002, and another for the Glasgow Bar Association when Simple Procedure was launched in 2016.

Andrew has written extensively on civil procedure and is a contributor to *Greens Litigation Styles*. He is the author of *Style Writs for the Sheriff Court* 5th edition (Bloomsbury, 2023) and *A Practical Guide to Conducting a Sheriff Court Proof* (Law Brief Publishing, 2023). He is a past President of the G.B.A. and was formerly a Reporter to the Client Relations Office of the Law Society of Scotland. He is currently the Secretary of the Scottish Law Agents' Society. Andrew is a columnist for *The Scotsman*. He has drafted legislation for the Church of Scotland and is a vice-convenor of its Discipline Tribunal.

A Practical Guide to Simple Procedure in the Sheriff Courts in Scotland

A Practical Guide to Simple Procedure in the Sheriff Courts in Scotland

Andrew Gordon Stevenson
Solicitor Advocate

Law Brief Publishing

Published 2025 by Law Brief Publishing, an imprint of Law Brief Publishing Ltd
30 The Parks
Minehead
Somerset
TA24 8BT

www.lawbriefpublishing.com

Paperback: 978-1-916698-68-0

PREFACE

Dobie on Sheriff Court Practice (1952) was a product of less frantic times. It devotes an easily digestible 28 pages to the Small Debt Court, a forum which encompassed a wider range of remedies than are competent under Simple Procedure. Around the same number of pages covers the latter in the current edition (2022) of *Macphail on Sheriff Court Practice*.

This book is different in tone and ambition to both those eminent works. It modestly endeavours to be more of a survival guide for the author's colleagues traversing the mine strewn landscape of the deceptively named Simple Procedure.

Pre-internet, books on court procedure often used to incorporate legislation. Now, that would be both a waste of paper and completely unnecessary given the easy access online to statutes and acts of sederunt. It would also entice readers into a false sense of security that the law is static and unchanging. Any reader of this book needs to regard it as a supplement to the Rules themselves as well as the other instruments mentioned herein. These evolve more often than they probably need to, at a pace detrimental to the practitioner who relies solely on textbooks and omits to investigate the law as at stands at the time when it matters.

Thanks to Garry Wright for all his help and patience in the preparation of this book.

The law is stated as at 1st January 2025.

Andrew Gordon Stevenson
Troon, South Ayrshire, January 2025

CONTENTS

TABLE OF CASES

Ackrim v UK Insurance Ltd [2024] SC EDIN 53

Alston v Macdougall (1887) 15 R 78

Barton v Wright Hassall LLP [2018] UKSC 12

Beattie v the Royal Bank of Scotland plc 2003 SLT 564

Bell v Farmer and Farmer [2023] SAC (Civ) 6

Black Horse Ltd v Cameron [2019] SC DUM 36, 2019 SLT (Sh Ct) 155

Nathan Blair v Heather Baird [2021] SAC (Civ)13

Bradford and Bingley v Rashid [2006] *UKHL 37*

Cabot Financial UK Ltd v Ryan Bell [2023] CSIH 43

Cabot Financial (UK) Ltd v Donnelly 2022 SLT (Sh Ct) 147

Cabot Financial (UK) Ltd v Finnegan 2021 SLT (Sh Ct) 237

Cabot Financial UK Ltd v Robert McGregor, Liam Gardner and Kirsty Brown [2018] SAC (Civ) 12

Clydesdale Financial Services Ltd v Wojcick [2019] SC PER 29

Norman Christie v Portman Motors [2024] SAC (Civ) 10

Churchill v Merthyr Tydfil County Borough Council [2023] EWCA Civ 1416

Jamie Davis v Skyfire Insurance [2019] SC EDIN 24

Doran V SC Causewayside Ltd [2023] SAC (Civ) 10

Douglas v Douglas [2020] SAC (Civ) 14

Dransfield and another v Information Commissioner (2016) 3 All E.R. 221

Dunhill v W Brook and Co [2016] EWHC 165 (Q.B.)

Dunn v Hall 1990 S.C.L.R. 673

Fellowes' Executor v Fellowes' Trustees 1988 SLT 730

Natalie Gowans v Elizabeth Miller [2017] SC FR 82

Ian Graham v Paul Farrell [2017] SC EDIN 75

Hamilton v Murray and Co (1830) 9 S 143

Hunter v Hanley 1955 SC 200

Japan Leasing (Europe) plc v Weir's Trustee (No 2) 1998 SC 543

KN v XD Inc [2024] NZDT 131

Karl Construction v Palisade Properties Plc SLT 2002 312

Kennedy v Cordia (Services) LLP [2016] UKSC 6

Khaliq v Gutowski 2019 SC 136

Kissner and Werner v McDonald's Corporation

Madden v Glasgow Corporation 1923 SC 102

Mazur v Primrose and Gordon [2015] CSIH 8

Andrew Martin v Southern Rock Insurance Co Ltd [2018] SC EDIN 10

McCandlish v Johnston and Sweeney 2024 SAC (Civ) 17

Milne v Uniroyal Englebert Tyres Ltd 1995 SLT (Sh Ct) 23

OB v CM [2021] NZDT 121

Ochiemhen v Secretary of State of the Home Department [2016] CSOH 20

Ashleigh Potter v OSC Group Ltd unreported 12th July 2017, Aberdeen Sheriff Court

Peter Cusack Property Consultancy Ltd v Simpson and others [2024] SC GLA 44.

Purves v Joydisc Ltd 2003 SLT (Sh Ct) 64

QT v B Ltd [2024] NZDT 148

Ravensby Glass Co Ltd v Lifestyle Glass Design Ltd [2019] SAC (Civ) 15

S v Argyll and Clyde Acute Hospitals NHS Trust [2009] CSOH 43

Santander Consumer (UK) Plc v Alan Creighton and *Santander Consumer (UK) Plc v William Simpson* [2019] SAC (Civ) 36

Scott v Scott 1913 A.C. 417

Scottish Woodlands Ltd v Majekodunmi and another [2019] SAC (Civ) 38

Slessor-Burnett v Stuart 1990 SLT (Sh Ct) 62

Sloan v Mycock 1992 SLT (Sh Ct) 23

Smith v Duncan [2022] SAC (Civ) 16

Sproll v Walker 1900 2F 73

Stevenson v Midlothian District Council 1983 SC(HL) 50

Unison v Lord Chancellor [2017] UKSC 51

Walkingshaw v Glenalmond Trading Industries Ltd [2024] SC PER 47

Paul Whyte v Troy Lucas (a firm and George Rusz [2019] EWHC 1098 QB

Winans v Macrae [1885] S.L.R. 22

2020 SC GLA 40

USE OF TERMINOLOGY

Care must be taken over the use of words and phrases in a book which examines court procedure, because many of them are terms of art. For example, simple procedure adopts specific meanings for "hearing" and "decision" which are at odds with how they are deployed and defined elsewhere in the Scottish civil courts. It omits important terms that are used in related legislation too. For example, section 110 of the Courts Reform Act 2014 allows appeals against a "final judgment" whereas the term "judgment" is absent from the Simple Procedure Rules, a point that the Sheriff Appeal Court had to resolve in *Bell v Farmer and Farmer* [2023] SAC (Civ) 6.

In discussing steps or stages of procedure I have tried to use neutral language. For instance, the word "diet" does not occur in the Simple Procedure Rules and it is used here to denote a calling in court.

I have tried to alternate singular gender pronouns and to avoid the ambiguity created by the use of the singular "they" to denote one individual. "They" is used here only to indicate plural.

To avoid repetition, in referring to the Simple Procedure Rules I have dispensed with the word "Rule", referring for example to "1.2" rather than "Rule 1.2". If the word "Rule" appears it is because the provision is not one of the Simple Procedure Rules, but it is of a different set, such as the Taxation of Judicial Expenses Rules 2019.

CHAPTER ONE

RISK MANAGEMENT

"*Simple Procedure is supposed to be simple and not difficult.*";

– Lord Carloway, Cabot Financial (UK) Ltd v Ryan Bell, 21st November 2023

"*The angst of a litigation is inversely proportional to its value*";

– a (cynical but shrewd) specialist sheriff in the All Scotland Sheriff Personal Injury Court

This book is a practical guide aimed at solicitors. There have been many books on court procedure but, alas, they have a tendency to pass over the omnipresent dangers of expense and complaints. For instance, it is all very well to write that a party may instruct an expert witness. The practitioner's initial questions should be; how much will that cost, who is ultimately going to foot the bill and will he be angry about it? Unfortunately, simple procedure possesses certain features which exacerbate the hazards to legal advisors. These are identified repeatedly throughout this book. From a risk management perspective it does no harm to recognise the disagreeable necessity of regarding every potential client as a name on a letter from the Scottish Legal Complaints Commission.

Firstly though, an important distinction requires to be drawn between the institutional client, i.e. a large organisation, and the type who raises or faces maybe one or two cases in her lifetime. The former would include property factors, utility suppliers and vehicle hire companies, where the claims are usually formulaic; only the name, dates and sum due are different. Such business may well be conducted by large legal companies engaging an army of paralegals working from home. As regards the latter type of clientele, many solicitors have had a private client who has a dispute over a breach of missives, a pet, a holiday from hell or a minor collision in a supermarket car park where insurers are not involved. She will look for advice on how or whether to raise an action or may arrive at the office anxiously clutching a recorded delivery envelope containing Forms 3D Timetable, 6A Notice of a Claim, 3A Claim Form, 5A Application for a Time to Pay Direction and 4A Response Form. She may be of the firm view that courts are for other people, not her.

In order to be most useful this book is focussed principally on the latter client because the solicitor who acts there is dealing with a unique and unfamiliar set of circumstances. These may be challenging. In this book it can be assumed that any reference to a client excludes the institutional variety unless the context indicates otherwise.

This book does not deal with the system that was introduced by the Act of Sederunt (Sheriff Court European Small Claims Procedure Rules) 2008 as amended.

It might seem odd to commence a book on simple procedure with some remarks about the law of diligence. However, putting oneself in the shoes of the client makes that topic an obvious and crucial subject for consideration. Litigation and diligence are equally essential components in the one exercise of debt recovery. Court lawyers need to be knowledgeable about both. Diligence is important both at the interim stage and after a decree has been obtained. It is dealt with in the Simple Procedure Rules under Parts 20 Provisional Orders and 15 How to Enforce a Decision respectively.

A simple procedure client – or any litigation client, or indeed any client – wants something tangible or at least concrete; a wad of cash (such as used to be handed over frequently by respondents in the sequestration court in Glasgow), a cheque that will not be dishonoured, a bank transfer of funds, an object or an item of property. He does not want;

i. A document telling him that he is entitled to the cash, cheque, transfer or object. He already knew that; he instructed the solicitor in order to gain the cash etc, not to obtain confirmation of the fact that he is due it.

ii. The solicitor's bill. By itself, that leaves him poorer than if he had never crossed the lawyer's threshold.

Any discussion with a client who wishes a solicitor to act for him in a simple procedure case requires that the latter explain some harsh truths and that, from a risk management perspective, there is a record in the file of the warnings having been given. These will include that;

A. It is uneconomical to instruct a lawyer, at least beyond the initial stages.

B. Suing someone with no money (or no accessible money) is a futile exercise.

C. Where the respondent (i.e. defender) is abroad it is probably best for the client to walk away, put it down to experience and be more careful in future dealings.

D. Litigation is inherently hazardous and unpredictable. Mistakes occur. If sheriffs were infallible there would be no need for appeal courts.

E. Nonetheless, rights of appeal are very limited. Although most court lawyers are able to frame an argument in terms of it's being a point of law there is nothing to be gained in employing this craft if the point actually hinges on an unappealable factor such as that a witness was not believed. In such circumstances one is simply wasting the time of the Sheriff Appeal Court and costing the client time and money.

F. The sheriff might not accept that the client's evidence or that of the client's witness is sufficiently reliable or credible. It is very common for someone to go into court and lose. Statistically there are about as many losers as winners. Very few people envisage that they will go into court only to be branded a knave or a fool (sometimes both), but that rude shock befalls someone every day.

G. The court will effectively wash its hands of a case once it has decided it on the merits and determined expenses. It will not take any part in enforcement unless actively engaged to do so by the raising of more proceedings. The claimant becomes a creditor and is on his own. Only in the criminal courts does Scottish Courts and Tribunals Service collect sums, including fines, due by the losing party but some clients will assume that this task is undertaken in relation to civil court decrees too.

It needs to be made abundantly clear too that just because a claim is modest in value it must not be assumed that the lawyer's fee will be small as well. There is absolutely no reason for a solicitor to charge a reduced fee for dealing with a low value claim. The potential loss and therefore the responsibility is less but the risk of a complaint is not.

Prior to the Solicitors (Scotland) Act 1988 a client who claimed that her lawyer had been negligent had to sue him and prove actual loss. Further, the courts have ruled that errors of judgment do not create liability unless the person under scrutiny has followed a course such that no professional person could have taken if acting with ordinary care; *Hunter v Hanley* 1955 SC 200.

However, this protection will be of use only if the client actually sues, and has the dispute tested in court. Solicitors face a hazard that is far more likely to materialise than a negligence case in the courts. The Solicitors (Scotland) Act 1988 created the concept of inadequate professional service (I.P.S.), which consists of "professional services which are in *any* respect not of the quality which could reasonably be expected of a competent solicitor" (italics added). Providing an I.P.S. entitles the client to complain. It even allows third parties to do so if they have been directly affected by the service. These are persons with whom the solicitor has no contractual relationship. Giving the power of complaint to one's own client's opponent can lead to absurd situations. There is currently a Scottish judge who had, whilst in private practice, been the subject of a S.L.C.C. complaint by his client's opponent whom he had cross-examined in a manner which had resulted in victory for the client but bitter resentment in the opponent. In other words, the judge had been too good at his job as a litigator. Although the complaint was unsuccessful the practitioner should never have had his time wasted in this way.

I.P.S. and the S.L.C.C. remove the protection afforded to the solicitor by *Hunter v Hanley* because clients can circumvent the courts completely and rely on an error as constituting an inadequacy of the service provided. By using the Commission's complaints procedure they save themselves the cost and risk of litigation.

Originally, all I.P.S. complaints were determined by the Law Society of Scotland. Nowadays such complaints are handled by the Commission. Its website is chatty and welcoming, with smiling cartoon figures. ("Hello, we're the S.L.C.C ... and our service is free"; to the complainer for sure but not to the legal profession which funds it). However, receiving a complaint is nothing to smile about.

Leaving aside the 1988 Act it is implied by the law of contract that a lawyer must provide a service of a reasonable standard. There is a delictual duty of care to do so too. So, the threat of court action by the client remains, as an additional peril for the practitioner.

This hazardous landscape means that if it takes at least three hours adequately to draft Forms, peruse evidence, speak to witnesses, prepare for hearings, compile submissions and so on then the solicitor is compelled to spend that time and should charge therefor. Doing less is risking a complaint or claim. On the other hand, lawyers can lose time and money dealing with low value actions in areas of law with which they are unfamiliar. They may have to spend perhaps two hours researching the law. Generally, such research is not chargeable to the client because lawyers are expected to know the law. There are other realities of which most members of the public are unaware; many high street solicitors do not have easy access to law libraries because of cost.

CHAPTER TWO

THE COSTS OF LOW VALUE ACTIONS

The cost to the taxpayer

In determining fees throughout the civil courts the Scottish Government and the English Ministry for Justice apply the principle of "full cost recovery" whereby court users are expected to pay for the litigation in which they are involved.

This approach treats litigants as service users in the same way as if they were having their bins emptied. It is completely misconceived. The correct view – which the government chooses to disregard – is reflected in the judgment issued by the Supreme Court in *Unison v Lord Chancellor* [2017] UKSC 51. Lord Reed's masterly explanation of the role of the civil courts in a civilised society should be read by every court practitioner, and also by the Scottish and U.K. Governments. They would learn, for example, that "Access to the courts is not .. of value only to the particular individuals involved."

To be fair, however, it has always been recognised, correctly, that the courts should not be consuming public funds in hearing matters that are of little or no importance. In a country where food banks have become the norm it is important to prioritise public spending.

Viscount Stair refers at p610 of his *Institutions* to the principle that *de minimis non curat praetor*, which is to say that a judge is not concerned with trifles. The dictum, derived from Roman law but recognised across English speaking jurisdictions, evolved over time to state that the law rather than the judge is not so concerned (*de minimis non curat lex*). Perhaps it ought to be modified again to state that the public purse ought not to be so concerned. Yet the principle, regardless of who ought not to be concerned, has never been applied in the Scottish courts other than in the context of *sponsiones ludicrae* (see below). Otherwise, judges would have been able to refuse to hear trivial cases. Instead, actions of low value have always been present in Scotland, and not always in what are jarringly described in the Rules of the Court of Session as "inferior" courts namely the sheriff court. *Walker on Damages* refers at page 21 to two Outer House delict actions, *Sproll v Walker* 1900 2F 73 and *Madden v Glasgow Corporation 1923 SC 102* in which the sum awarded was one farthing i.e. a quarter of 1d.

Unrestricted access to justice has always had its critics. Sir Walter Scott, who was sheriff of Selkirk two hundred years ago, thought that;

"too cheap access to litigation has its evils ..., for the proneness of the lower classes to gratify spite and revenge in this way would be a dreadful evil were they able to endure the expense. . Wretched wranglings about a few pounds, begun in spleen, and carried on from obstinacy, and at length fear of the conclusion to the banquet of ill-humour, Damnation of Expenses." (*Journal* entry, 12th December 1825).

Perhaps the most famously frivolous and inconsequential Scottish case is *Winans v Macrae* [1885] S.L.R. 22, in which a landowner sought interdict to stop a neighbour's lamb straying onto his 200,000 acre estate. "We will protect a man against his right being trespassed on, but not against children toddling on the land at the roadside, or against a dog or kitten going on it. If the pursuer wishes to exclude these things he must get the means himself, and not apply to Her Majesty's Judges for interdict against them" said a clearly exasperated Lord Young. No doubt his Lordship would have liked to have sent the pursuer packing. However, at each stage of the dispute the sheriff then the sheriff principal and lastly the Inner House all had no option but to hear and to try to determine the case.

The principle *de minimis non curat lex* is not applied in foreign litigation either. It was certainly not implemented in *Kissner and Werner v McDonald's Corporation*, a 2018 case in the District Court of the

Southern District of Florida. The issue there was whether the defendant had been unjustly enriched by having served cheeseburgers from which the cheese had been removed (at the customers' own request) but then having charged the cheese averse customers the same price as for a standard cheeseburger. Had the *de minimis* concept been applied that claim, which was unsuccessful, would never have been entertained.

True, *de minimis non curat lex* has been the justification for the Scottish courts refusing to hear cases concerning gambling contracts. Such an agreement is known as a *sponsio ludicra.* This would include, for example, a simple procedure claim over an office syndicate in which the participants agree to share the winning of a weekly lottery and in which the victor reneges. However, it is arguable that any refusal to entertain a claim arising from such an arrangement infringes the citizen's rights under section 1 and Article 6 of Schedule 1 of the Human Rights Act 1998 (of which more below). Perhaps recognising this point, section 335 of the Gambling Act 2005 stipulates that the "fact that a contract relates to gambling shall not prevent its enforcement."

It would be contrary to Article 6 to fail to provide any forum for the resolution of disputes of a minimal amount. The individual is entitled to seek a remedy. Also, it would not be in the public interest. It would mean that unscrupulous credit providers, car parking companies and others could act with impunity in levying small but dubious charges against hundreds or thousands of people, raking in substantial ill-gotten gains. If there were to be a sum below which it was incompetent to sue, such as £50, not only would their victims have no means of redress but the perpetrators' questionable conduct could not be checked.

Incidentally, a recognition of the *de minimis* principle can be found in clause 26.1 of the Scottish Standard Clauses (6th edition). This precludes a house buyer from suing for claims "in aggregate to less than £500". That ought to eliminate from simple procedure the most trivial breach of missives actions over blown light bulbs and the like. Obviously, however, this is a contractual waiver of rights to sue. Without it such actions would be perfectly competent.

Courts are public authorities and are obliged to have regards to Article 6. This is often described as the clause entitled the citizen to a fair trial. In the context of Scottish civil law this is not the whole story. In the English courts and in those of countries whose legal system is based on that of England, "trial" includes the evidence hearing stage of a civil claim as well as that of a criminal prosecution. Of course, the Scottish system describes the former as a proof (although not under simple procedure). Article 6 uses "trial" in the English sense, covering both civil and criminal cases. In other words, Article 6 applies to proofs in the Scottish courts and to simple procedure in general. This entitles one to a fair determination of one's rights and obligations within a reasonable time in a public forum.

Often, it is useful to see the approach and opinions of other jurisdictions which face exactly the same issues as we do. The Law Reform Commission of the Canadian province of Manitoba reported on 7th March 1983 on The Adjudication of Smaller Claims and identified the "need to be mindful that the costs in administering small claims must be balanced against the objective of providing an accessible and effective court that is procedurally fair and governed by the rule of law. The ultimate goal in forming a small claim court therefore is to find the "point of equilibrium" between these somewhat countervailing factors." (p6). This same is true in Scotland.

In small value actions there can be a trade-off between, on the one hand, speed, low cost and informality and, on the other hand, reaching the correct decision. Generally, it will be cheaper to lead inferior evidence. In New South Wales, witness statements are lodged instead of that evidence being in the form of parole testimony given in a witness box. In South Africa cross-examination is not allowed. That prohibition will obviously curtail procedure, saving time and therefore money. That is the *quid pro quo.*

Some systems, such as that in South Africa, forbid legal representation. However, if lawyers are absent there is a saving of money but an increased risk of a miscarriage of justice because party litigants are not legally qualified and are therefore not fully aware of their rights.

None of this is intended to be critical of the systems of New South Wales or South Africa. It is simply an observation that litigating inexpensively, quickly and informally risks jeopardising the quality of justice dispensed. Clearly that will not inevitably occur in every case, but it will happen in some of them, and if one of them happened to be one's own there would be a feeling of grievance. Arguably, however, that is a price worth paying. Nobody can justify spending thousands of pounds of taxpayers' money (a sheriff's salary and other court costs as well as legal aid) on, for example, a dispute over a faulty dishwasher or a garden gnome.

It is easy to see why the courts are so enthusiastic to see disputes resolved by settlement or by A.D.R. (alternative dispute resolution, such as mediation or arbitration);

1. It saves taxpayers' money.
2. It devolves to somebody else, and thereby removes from the courts, the responsibility of reaching decisions based on inferior material, whether that be evidence or representations. When a case settles the winner's right is based on a contract (namely the settlement) and not on a court's decision. The integrity and reliability of a court's decision is only as good as the material with which it is presented. "Summary justice" generally carries bad connotations; one thinks of the rough and ready decision-making doled out by a 16th century Scottish baron, the type more concerned with order than with law.

<u>The cost to the litigant</u>

From the practitioner's perspective this is far more important than the cost to the taxpayer. The simple procedure litigant who instructs a solicitor beyond the initial stage is going to lose money. For the lawyer's own protection, if for no other reason, this needs to be spelt out in a clear and verifiable manner.

Firstly, there is the relatively safe issue of outlays, payable by the litigant whether legally represented or not.

To raise the action the claimant must pay court fees to the sheriff clerk. These are determined by the Sheriff Court Fees Order 2024.

Relative to those in the ordinary court these fees are modest. As of 1st November 2024 they are as follows;

To commence an action for £300 or less the fee is £22.

If the claim is for more than £300 that fee is £123.

If the sheriff clerk is requested under 6.11(2) to effect service of the Claim Form and has to instruct a sheriff officer the claimant will have to pay £14 plus the officer's bill. The Order is silent regarding the far more complicated question of the costs of service under Part 19 (where the respondent is outwith Scotland).

The claimant or respondent marking an appeal under Part 16 incurs a fee of £72.

By contrast, for small claims in England (which can be up to £10,000 rather than £5000 as here) there are seven bands of initial court fees, from £35 to £455 depending on the value of the claim. In addition, there are further fees at later stages.

In Ontario, a "frequent claimant", filing more than ten small claims a year, pays more than twice as much per case than an infrequent one, inverting the principle that a bulk customer should obtain a discount. In New South Wales a corporate claimant pays more than one who is an individual.

S.C.T.S. make provision for the poor to be exempted from paying these court fees. If such claimants are lucky there will be no further outlays to meet. Alas, so often a claimant will be required to meet further outlays which dwarf these court fees. These will be mentioned later in this book but suffice to say that sheriff officers, witnesses (Part 11), commissioners (Part 10), process servers, *huissiers*, interpreters and shorthand writers are not cheap. In simple procedure these outlays may well be utterly disproportionate to the value of the claim to the point of making it unviable.

In 2001, as a Reporter to the Law Society's euphemistically named Client Relations Office, the author recommended that the committee uphold a complaint flowing from an ordinary action in which the client sought contact to his child. He had been advised by his solicitor that the cost would be in the region of £2000. The sheriff appointed a child welfare reporter to investigate. The eventual bill was £9340 of which the invoice of the reporter, a solicitor in private practice, was £8490. The committee found that there had been I.P.S. The moral is that the solicitor must warn the client in advance of the possible magnitude of outlays and emphasise the worst-case scenario.

Secondly, there is the issue of solicitors' fees.

Solicitors are obliged to advise clients about legal aid even if they do not offer it themselves, because the client may then choose to go to another firm which does. Legal aid is available under simple procedure although whether that is a good thing is debatable if the aim is to discourage legal representation. It would be better for the profession if legal aid were to be confined to ordinary and summary cause actions. The system imposes upon the solicitor a raft of administrative tasks and responsibilities which do not concern the agents of private payers, such as the time-consuming completion of forms, estimating and adhering to a cost ceiling, obtaining sanction for expenditure, advising the Scottish Legal Aid Board on settlement offers and a myriad of other unremunerative requirements. Often, legal aid does not work too well for clients either. Space does not allow a discussion here of the consequences of "clawback". Suffice to say that it applies in all levels of court action, proportionately of more significance in lower value claims.

The availability of legal aid in simple procedure mirrors the position as it applied prior to 2016 when there was small claim procedure for actions of £3000 and below and summary cause procedure for actions worth above £3000 but not more than £5000. Broadly speaking, legal aid was available for the latter but not the former.

Incidentally, the current legislation is potentially confusing. Section 14 of the Legal Aid (Scotland) Act 1986 is headed "Availability of civil legal aid". Rule 3A of Part II ("excepted proceedings") of Schedule 2 to the Act provides that legal aid is not available for the following categories of simple procedure claim;

(a) For a sum of money not exceeding £3000 except aliment or interim aliment and actions for personal injury

(b) Those a*d factum praestandum* or for recovery of moveable property where there is an alternative crave for money not exceeding £3000.

The first branch tends to suggest that it is competent to pursue a simple procedure claim for aliment or personal injury, and that legal aid is available in principle to do so. This is not the case, however. These types of action must be brought as summary causes if they are worth £5000 or less. The reason why is based in obscure commencement provisions (see below).

If the client is to fund the case privately rather than under legal aid a different set of challenges arises. Some clients are able to obtain funding under their home insurance policy. This creates extra administration for the solicitor and the hourly rates payable are usually inadequate, to be treated as a contribution rather than covering the whole cost. The author is currently engaged in a complex and high value ordinary action where the insurers will pay only a miserly £120 per hour. The client will make up the considerable shortfall. It is imperative to advise the client that he is the contracting party and retains the principal obligation to pay the fees.

The issue of expenses is dealt with later in this book. It is worth emphasising at this point that solicitors need to get and to maintain adequate funding at all times if they are not to risk having to raise their own simple procedure claim for payment of fees subsequently.

It has already been mentioned that it is not economical to instruct a solicitor to conduct a simple procedure case. That applies both to pursuing and defending an action. It is easy to see why. Assume that the solicitor's fees are £250 per hour including VAT. It is not difficult to reach £500; all it takes is a 40-minute meeting, two 10 minute telephone calls, some email correspondence, perusing a few documents, taking a precognition and preparing the terms of a claim form or response. That is before the lawyer even contacts the court or opponent.

One of the greatest differences between court work and private client business is that only the latter can be treated as a commodity to be packaged and priced in advance. There is transparency and predictability from the outset. The lawyer's practice can produce a set of charges, a menu which lists the fee for a will, codicil, power of attorney, discharge of a standard security, conveyance, guardianship and so on. Preparation of a codicil might be charged at £125 including VAT, half an hour's work. Court lawyers know that this model cannot be applied to litigation unless the case is to be a "loss leader" or where the solicitor takes the "swings and roundabouts" approach with regular clients with repeat business.

The costs of running a lawyer's office will be the same per hour regardless of how remunerative the work being undertaken. It matters not whether a court action is worth £4000, £40,000 or £400,000. These costs include staff salaries, rent, business rates, stationery, insurance, practising certificate fee, S.L.C.C levy and so on. None of these burdens will be diminished by the value of the ongoing litigation.

Space does not allow full consideration of the insidious principle of "no win, no fee". It is a bonus for personal injury lawyers who can cherry pick clients who have been injured through no fault of theirs. For other court lawyers, indeed the majority of them, it has generated numerous problems. Chief amongst them is the twisted proposition that if a client loses a case his or her lawyer is not deserving of a fee. This is why it is so crucial that solicitors obtain funds in advance. Otherwise, there is the risk of encountering that bane of court practice, the client who is disbelieved by the sheriff, loses his case and then blames the lawyer and complains to the S.L.C.C. in the expectation that the lawyer will knock a chunk off the bill to avoid countless hours of wasted time and energy. Unfortunately, because this tactic carries no risk or cost to the client it is often a successful ploy.

No win no fee carries all manner of implications none of which is good for the profession. It implies that a lawyer needs the incentive of a bonus to do her job properly. It invites the notion that if it is reasonable in principle for lawyers to share in the spoils when a claim is successful they should all bear some of the loss when it is not, regardless of whether they signed up to such an arrangement or not and without any consideration of how challenging the case happens to be. It is a deterrent to lawyers agreeing to act in tricky cases, which is hardly in the public interest.

Inextricably linked to the economies of instructing a solicitor are the questions of

(a) how much the court can allow in recoverable costs in the event of success and,

(b) will the opponent be good for the money or be a penniless thing of straw?

In other words, what is the law regarding expenses and diligence? The former is dealt with at length below but of these the latter is more important in obtaining a practical outcome for the client. That is so both in relation to interim diligence (preserving the opponent's assets *ad interim*) and accessing them in the event of a successful conclusion to the action.

Clients are entitled to be fully advised on all these matters before they can make an informed decision on whether or not to go to the cost and trouble of raising an action at all. A fundamental aim of litigation and diligence is to become enriched and not impoverished by the experience. The client who thinks that the only beneficiary of his case is his own lawyer is likely to harbour resentment.

Whereas rules on court procedure generally run chronologically, an awareness of diligence means looking at the end of the process and working back from that, anti-chronologically.

It is insufficiently broadcast by S.C.T.S that the courts will provide no assistance whatsoever in enforcing a decree.

The Diligence Working Group Report of March 2021 on the Review of Diligence in Scotland recommended that the Scottish Civil Justice Council be asked to consider updating the Simple Procedure Claim Form 3A – the equivalent of an initial writ – to reflect that "it is important that simple procedure guidance highlights that a successful simple procedure claim does not necessarily mean that the debt will be recovered." The Form 3A still fails to provide this warning, one that ought to be included.

The objective of a simple procedure claim – and indeed of any litigation – is to gain an effective remedy. There is no point in spending money to obtain a court order entitling one to extract blood from a stone.

Some remedies can be granted by the court without any enforcement, such as declarators and divorce, but these are the exception. Even interdicts need to be served in order to be effective.

There is no kind of simple procedure remedy (payment, delivery of moveable property or orders *ad factum praestandum*) which is effective without being enforced. They all require a piece of paper – or electronic document – which satisfies a sheriff officer that he can take steps to recover a debt. Such steps include serving a charge for payment or arresting a bank account.

No book on the practice of simple procedure can fail to omit consideration of the dismal reality that is the law of diligence in Scotland.

In 1988, the year in which small claims procedure was introduced, a decree could be implemented by carrying out a poinding, i.e. by sheriff officers seizing a debtor's moveable property. This was then followed up by a warrant sale, whereby the officer would sell the property in order to raise money to pay the creditor. Poindings worked and so did the threat of a warrant sale. In the years that the author instructed sheriff orders to poind goods and arrange warrant sales no sale ever required to go ahead. Without exception, the debtor found the way to pay up, often by borrowing from family.

However, since 1988 politicians in Scotland have increasingly tended to regard debtors as victims. The Abolition of Poindings and Warrant Sales Act 2001 was introduced by the Scottish Socialist Party. It was short – just 4 sections long – and put absolutely nothing in place of this diligence. Subsequent legislation created watered down versions of these provisions, which are examined later in this book. These are to the detriment of creditors including not just big companies but individual victims of wrongdoing and other ordinary citizens due compensation. There is now a vast section of the population which it is simply not worth suing because a decree will be valueless.

Another development that has occurred since 1988 is that more people care less about being the subject of a court order for payment. A generation existed then which would have found it embarrassing to be taken to court and ordered to pay a debt. That demographic stratum has now passed on, and a lot more of the public feel no stigma in being a bad payer, contract breaker or a defaulter.

It is understandable that many clients assume that at no cost to themselves, the court has staff who will recover the money awarded to them under a decree in the same way as the S.C.T.S. Fines Enforcement Team collects funds from offenders. This misconception is not restricted to Scotland. Consider the following observations from Manitoba, for example;

> "The inability of judgment creditors to enforce small claims judgments has been a common complaint here and in other jurisdictions. Individuals are often aware that the onus is on them to realize on their judgments, and the proceedings can be complicated and frustrating to self-represented litigants."
>
> – Manitoba Law Reform Commission Report, 7th March 1983, p43. canlii.org. bit.ly/408IGyh

Fifteen years later the same problem remained (and still does);

> "Ultimately, however, it is up to the judgment creditor, and not the court, to enforce the judgment. Many individual claimants fail to realize this fact before filing their claim, and are subsequently disappointed."
>
> "No province appears to have managed to provide an enforcement mechanism that succeeds so as to relieve the frustration and aggravation experienced by so many small claims judgment creditors".
>
> – Report by Manitoba Law Reform Commission 17th March 1998, pp11 and 48 http://www.manitobalawreform.ca/pubs/pdf/fullreports/99-full_report.pdf

CHAPTER THREE

SOURCES OF THE LAW OF SIMPLE PROCEDURE

Belying the notion that the system is simple its sources are numerous and, for a procedure intended to be readily comprehensible to party litigants, convoluted.

The procedure is to be found in various repositories. These can be classified under the following headings;

1. The Courts Reform (Scotland) Act 2014.

This primary legislation is the constitution of simple procedure, which is defined by section 72 *et seq.* and regulated by section 104. By contrast, that of ordinary and summary cause procedure is the Sheriff Courts (Scotland) Act 1907 section 39 and the Sheriff Courts (Scotland) Act 1971 sections 32 and 35 respectively. The 2014 Act also created the office of summary sheriff and it established the Sheriff Appeal Court both of which are integral parts of the simple procedure system.

2. The Act of Sederunt (Simple Procedure) 2016, No. 200

The basis for this secondary legislation is section 104 of the 2014 Act, which allows the Court of Session to regulate procedure in the sheriff court. Note that there is a crucial difference between these "Regulations" themselves, of which there are currently five, and the twenty "Rules", which are derived from Regulation 2 and which are contained within Schedule 1 to the Regulations. These Rules are analysed in depth later in this book. There are also Forms in this Act of Sederunt.

Regulation 3 is headed "Interpretation of the Simple Procedure Rules" and refers to the following primary legislation (as well as to the 2014 Act). These are listed here alphabetically;

- Children (Scotland) Act 1995 section 11(1)(d)
- Civil Jurisdiction and Judgments Act 1982 Schedule 2, Articles 1 and 3
- Consumer Credit Act 1974 section 129
- Contracts (Applicable Law) Act 1990 Schedule 3 Articles 1 and 2
- Debt Arrangement and Attachment (Scotland) Act 2002 sections 9A(1), 9M(2), 9M(4), 9N(1) and 9N(3)
- Debtors (Scotland) Act 1987 sections 1 and 5 and 15A(1),15K(2), 15K(4), 15L(1) and 15L(3)
- Equality Act 2010 section 114(1)
- European Communities Act 1972 schedule 1 Part II
- Law Reform (Miscellaneous Provisions) (Scotland) Act 1990 sections 25 and 27.
- Solicitors (Scotland) Act 1980 sections 4 and 5
- Vulnerable Witnesses (Scotland) Act 2004 sections 12(2), 12(6), 13, 19 and 22(1)

As well as this primary legislation above, Regulation 3 refers to the following secondary legislation, listed here alphabetically;

- All-Scotland Sheriff Court (Sheriff Personal Injury Court) Order 2015

- Diligence (Scotland) Regulations 2009 regulation 3(1)(a) and Schedule 1

- Ordinary Cause Rules 1993

Also, Regulation 3 mentions the following two provisions of international law;

- The Convention of 15 November 1965 on the Service Abroad of Judicial and Extrajudicial Documents in Civil or Commercial Matters [Hague Convention]

- Regulation (EC) No 1393/2007 of the European Parliament and the Council of 13 November 2007 on the service in the Member States of judicial and extrajudicial documents in civil or commercial matters ... (Service Regulation]

This latter provision was revoked by the Service of Documents and Taking of Evidence in Civil and Commercial Matters (Revocation and Saving Provisions) (EU Exit) Regulations 2018 (S.I. 2018/1257). In remaining within Regulation 3 the Service Regulation is as anachronistic as the E.U. flag which still, inexplicably, flies outside the Scottish Parliament.

3. <u>The Simple Procedure Rules (derived from Regulation 2(1) of and comprising Schedule 1 to the Regulations)</u>

These Rules – of which more below – refer to the following statutes, listed here alphabetically;

- Bankruptcy and Diligence (Scotland) Act 2007 section 148(3)(b)

- Debt Arrangement and Attachment (Scotland) Act 2002 Part 1A section 9A(1)

- Debtors (Scotland) Act 1987 Part 1A, section 15A(1)

- Equality Act 2010 section 114

- Execution of Diligence (Scotland) Act 1926 sections 2 and 3

Also, the Rules refer to the following statutory instruments;

- Act of Sederunt (Sheriff Appeal Court Rules) 2021 S.S.I. 468

- Diligence (Scotland) Regulations 2009

- Rules for Applications in the Sheriff Court under the Debt Arrangement and Attachment Scotland) Act 2002

Mention should be made of Rule 21, a **Glossary** which states that it "contains a guide ... to the meaning of certain legal words and expressions" used in the Rules. There is then a table containing forty such words and expressions. Rule 21 is not a rule as such.

The Glossary is of questionable value. It is distinct and quite separate from Regulation 3 of the Act of Sederunt, which is entitled "Interpretation of the Simple Procedure Rules." So to locate a simple procedure definition one has to look in two places, namely Regulation 3 and Rule 21.

The Glossary is stated to be a "guide for litigants, lay representatives and courtroom supporters" This is misleading to them because it fails to either mention Regulation 3 or replicate its content. A good example of this is that whereas "a case where the expenses of a claim are capped" is defined in Regulation 3 as being one to which Section 81(1) of the 2014

Act applies this definition (which would be helpful) is completely absent from the Glossary.

The Summary Cause Glossary is superior, for four reasons;

1. It warns the reader that it is not definitive; the Summary Cause Glossary, at Rule 1.1(5) and Appendix 2, concerns "certain legal expressions ... but is not meant to be taken as giving those expressions any meaning which they do not have in law generally"

2. It deploys grammar; compare the following;

   - "Defender; person against whom a summary cause is started" as against

   - "Respondent; The person a claim is made against".

   The preposition "against" looks sloppy at the end of this statement. Perhaps this inelegance typifies the forcing of informality into an otherwise formal process. The dumbing down of language in official documents, such as court rules, is an unfortunate and rather defeatist tendency. According to the S.L.C.C.'s website "The average reading age in Scotland is 11. That means that the use of legal jargon and complex language is most likely going to result in a confused, unhappy client. Or a complaint." The Scottish Government states that the average reading age is "9-11 years old" Certainly, a lot of the simple procedure appears to have been aimed at the average primary 6 school pupil. Unfortunately, there are few such pupils who could navigate their way around the rules of expenses or diligence.

   The solution with court rules is not to abandon legal terms but to avoid poor English instead. Some court users will feel patronised, others that the drafting is merely amateurish.

3. It is more reliable. Part 21 contains a few dubious entries;

- "Dismissing a claim" is defined as "ending the case without deciding which party has been successful". That is plainly wrong; the respondent has been successful.

- "Recall" is said to be "An order cancelling a decision made by the sheriff", but that definition could apply equally well to the outcome of an appeal, not a recall. Instead, "Appeal" is defined as "Asking the Sheriff Appeal Court to reverse or vary the decision of a sheriff on a point of law".

The participant who is known in ordinary and summary cause procedure as a "third party" is defined by 4.4(2) as "additional respondent". The Glossary's definition, of a respondent "who enters the case later" is misleading. A third party is not the same as an additional defender. The Summary Cause Rules recognise this and include a whole Chapter 11 on third party procedure. Simple procedure should do likewise.

Instead, to confuse matters further, "third party" in simple procedure means a haver.

4. Although both sets of rules contain two provisions dealing with definitions, the vast bulk of the Summary Cause terms are in its Glossary. By contrast, there is a far more balanced split between Regulation 3 and Rule 21. This is unnecessary and cumbersome.

   There is duplication. "Trading name" is defined in the Glossary as being "A name under which a person, partnership or company carries out its business" and in Regulation 3 as "the trading or descriptive name of a person, partnership, limited liability partnership or company."

On a wider point, given that it was considered appropriate to add a Glossary to the Simple Procedure Rules it is inexplicable why it was decided to abandon terms such as pursuer, defender, third party, sist, proof in favour of claimant, respondent, additional respondent, pause, hearing and so on.

It is not asking a great deal for litigants to learn a few terms and phrases such as sist or proof. It is no more onerous than a holiday maker memorising a few words of conversational Spanish or French such as "Where is the beach?" or "Two beers please, waiter".

Furthermore, the traditional terms are time tested and are conducive to clearer thinking.

The Summary Cause Glossary includes; Pursuer; the person who starts a summary cause.

The Simple Procedure Glossary's equivalent is; Claimant; the person making a claim. The word "Pursuer" would have been equally intelligible.

The system of courts in Scotland is supposed to be unitary; cases may be remitted between the Court of Session and the sheriff court, ordinary to summary or simple procedure and *vice versa*. It makes no sense to have different terms to describe the same parties or processes. It would have been better to have included a glossary which translated terms such as to show that "application" equates to "motion", and so on.

4. The Simple Procedure Forms (derived from Regulation 1 of and Schedule 2 to the Regulations)

The Forms refer to the following Acts;

- Children (Scotland) Act 1995 sections 1(3), 11(3) and 13.
- Consumer Credit Act 1974
- Debt Arrangement and Attachment (Scotland) Act 2002 sections 9A(1,) 9D(2), 9E(3) and 9M

- Debtors (Scotland) Act 1987 sections 15A(1), 15E(2), 15F(3), 15F, 73F, 73F(2), 73F(4), 73F(5), 73G, 73H and 15K

- Vexatious Litigants (Scotland) Act 1898 [which was repealed by the 2014 Act; see section 100.] The S.C.T.S. website currently lists 13 such individuals.

- Vulnerable Witnesses (Scotland) Act 2004 sections 15(3)(a), 15(3)(b) and 11(2)

Also, the Forms refer to the Diligence (Scotland) Regulations 2009, Schedule 8.

Simple procedure is template based, more so than small claims procedure which made provision for such items as incidental applications, i.e. motions. These largely resembled those in ordinary procedure. By contrast, with the exception of a few documents such as Tenders, everything in simple procedure is intended to be capable of being fitted into one of the Forms. As will be discussed later, the format of the Forms is a means by which the procedure itself is governed._

5. Statutes not referred to in the Regulations or Rules, including but by no means limited to;

- Adults with Incapacity (Scotland) Act 2000 sections 15 and 57

- Children (Scotland) Act 1995 section 13

- Equality Act 2006, section 30(2)

- Judicial Factors Act 1849

- Prescription and Limitation (Scotland) Act 1973.

- Scottish Commission for Human Rights Act 2006

6. Secondary Legislation not referred to in the Regulations or Rules

- Small Claims (Scotland) Order 1988
- Sheriff Court Simple Procedure (Limits on Award of Expenses) Order 2016 SSI 2016/388
- Sheriff Court Simple Procedure (Limits on Award of Expenses) Amendment Order 2019 SSI 2019/79

7. Practice Notes

The Sheriff Principals' Guidance for Court Users, Electronic submission of documents, 14th October 2022

8. The common law

There are many procedural matters which are not governed by any primary or secondary legislation, most importantly;

Tenders. There is nothing in the Regulations or Rules about the lodging of a Tender. The Rules of the Court of Session omit any mention too. However, it is perfectly competent to tender in simple procedure just as it was in small claims. It occurred in *Ian Graham v Paul Farrell* [2017] SC EDIN 75 leaving the court having to hear an argument on how the question of expenses was affected. Incidentally, there is no reason for party litigants or lay representatives to be acquainted with the practice of Tenders that the amount tendered is not to be disclosed to the court in advance of acceptance or a final judgment. If lodging a Tender in a case in which the claimant is not legally represented it would be worth advising the opponent of this practice. Otherwise, there is a good chance that he will let the cat out of the bag.

On a similar point, it is highly unlikely that the average party litigant will know that correspondence marked "Without Prejudice" should not generally be disclosed to the court. The law on this topic was explored by the House of Lords in *Bradford and Bingley v Rashid* [2006] UKHL 37. Practitioners should be alert to the dangers of settlement proposals and "off the record" concessions being broadcast by unrepresented parties. These are the hazards when embroiled in a court process which has been designed to facilitate and encourage the participation of party litigants. Professional colleagues can (generally) be trusted to adhere to protocol about non- disclosure of settlement discussions. Litigants in person, as they are sometimes known, cannot. Unfortunately, this can be a deterrent against the negotiation that simple procedure professes to encourage.

Related to the Tender is the Pursuer's Offer. In the sheriff court this is an entirely a creature of legislation, namely Chapter 27A of the Ordinary Cause Rules. It is absent from summary cause and simple procedure. However, it is certainly worth considering whether such an offer might not be made in correspondence whilst litigating under simple procedure. The sheriff has considerable discretion over expenses and there is no reason why an offer to settle might not be founded upon where the respondent fails to beat the offer.

<u>Arrestment to found jurisdiction</u>. This is a rare occurrence in the sheriff court generally. Regulation 5 states that execution of such arrestment must be followed by service within 21 days. Schedule 8 rule 2(h) of the 1982 Act allows its use where the respondent is not domiciled in the U.K.; *Macphail* 9.105; a warrant to arrest to found jurisdiction must be made in a crave and the claimant needs to aver justification. So, this must be incorporated into the Simple Procedure Application Form 3A.

<u>Sisting of a mandatory</u>; this is an important safeguard where a party is overseas and liable to evade practical responsibility to pay expenses in the event of her losing the case. There is nothing about this in the simple procedure rules. The remedy is entirely within the discretion of the court; *Fellowes' Executor v Fellowes' Trustees* 1988 SLT 730.

<u>Caution for Expenses</u>; this is another wholly discretionary remedy; *Stevenson v Midlothian District Council* 1983 SC(HL) 50. It is founded

in common law other than that section 726 of the Companies Act 1985 applies to limited company claimants.

Dominis Litis; This is a person standing behind a nominal party but exerting *de facto* control. This might be John Falstaff the sole director and shareholder of John Falstaff Ltd. The court can order the lodging of caution for expenses or have the *dominis litis* found liable for expenses. Either way, there is nothing about this in the Simple Procedure Rules. Neither is there anything about those other two common law characters the *amicus curiae* or the *curator ad litem*.

Common law Abandonment; in *Beattie v the Royal Bank of Scotland plc* 2003 SLT 564 Lord Reed held that the existence of R.C.S.29 did not imply that common law abandonment had been rendered incompetent in the Court of Session. *Macphail* 14.22 deals with the process in the Ordinary Court. It is available under simple procedure too. In *Norman Christie v Portman Motors* [2024] SAC (Civ) 10 abandonment was made at the bar; with reference to *Macphail* 14.23 the appeal court held that this was competent.

Dropping a case from the Roll; Under Ordinary Procedure cases may be put on the back burner by two methods; they can drop from the roll or be sisted. Dropping from the roll will happen if, for example, a sist is recalled but no further order is made. This could be intentional or not. The Simple Procedure Rules appear to wish to discourage that which would amount to a *de facto* sist.

Agent withdrawing from acting; there are rules R.C.S 30.2 in the Court of Session and Chapter 24 of the Ordinary Cause rules providing for the assigning of a peremptory diet. There is no specific provision under simple procedure.

Remit to a person of skill; There is a specific rule for this under summary cause procedure (rule 8.4) but, surprisingly, none in simple procedure. It is submitted below that this mechanism is not a form of A.D.R. Such a remit can be a very efficient and cost-effective way of obtaining a determination of a technical point. It avoids the need for the parties to engage their own skilled witnesses. Small Claim Rule 1988 13.9 concerned remit to an appropriate person and the 2002 Rule 9.5 allowed a remit to determine a matter of fact; parties had to agree and were then bound by the decision of the person to whom the remit was made. Under the heading "Economy in litigation" the Supreme Court stated in *Kennedy v Cordia* (Services) LLP [2016] UKSC 6 that "a court which has case management powers can ascertain the scope for instruction of a single expert." That appears to encourage the sheriff to endeavour to persuade such an instruction in simple procedure.

Transference to an executor or representative on death or incapacity of the pursuer. Summary Cause Rule 15 covers these scenarios. Ordinary Cause Rules 25.1 and 25.2 were incorporated into small claims procedure. Simple procedure is silent. Again, this is surprising. It is not that uncommon for someone to die or lose capacity mid-litigation.

Interpreters; the practice of the courts in Scotland is that in civil actions the attendance of an interpreter is a matter for the party or witness who cannot understand English. There is nothing about them in the Regulations or Rules of simple procedure. *Macphail* 16.65 states that it is up to the sheriff to decide whether an interpreter is necessary and that interpreters must take the oath *de fideli administratione.* The court will not fund them of course, and they can be expensive.

CHAPTER FOUR

CIVIL ONLINE

Simple Procedure came into existence on 28th November 2016. It had been intended by S.C.T.S. that an online case management system would be operational then. The launch was delayed due to issues over testing. The author attended a Focus Group meeting at Parliament House on 14th August 2017 at which representatives of large debt recovery firms were present, eager to ensure that their software systems would be compatible with those of the court in order to create a seamless system. Civil Online was finally launched on 25th April 2019 in terms of the Act of Sederunt (Simple Procedure Amendment) Civil Online Order 2019 No. 122. Court users were not compelled to use the system. Plenty did, however. In the 20th May 2019 *Journal of the Law Society of Scotland* it was reported by S.C.T.S. that cases were being submitted at weekends. The report advised that there were around 35,000 simple procedure claims raised annually, this being a third of all actions in the sheriff court. This was expected to rise to around half when Special Simple Procedure Claims were introduced, although that was envisaged as including housing claims.

This optional nature of Civil Online changed when, following upon the arrival of Covid-19, the opportunity was taken to make it mandatory to lodge Claim Forms electronically as opposed to by hand, recorded delivery post or by using the Civil Portal on the S.C.T.S. website. This change was wrought by the Act of Sederunt (Simple Procedure Amendment) (Civil Online) Order 2020. That measure had a sunset clause imposing a time limit of six months. This was extended from 30th September 2021 to 31st March 2022 on which date the requirement was made permanent by the Act of Sederunt (Simple Procedure Amendment) (Civil Online) Order 2022. There is the possibility of exemption; if a claimant feels that he cannot submit the Form electronically he can ask the court to allow it to be done in person or by sending it in. Reasons must be provided. The decision is within the sheriff's discretion

A new Civil Online system became operational on 31st May 2023.

There are two User Guides, dated July 2024. One is aimed at party litigants -and covers simple procedure only – and the other is for solicitors. The contents of the latter illustrate how the intention is clearly to roll out Civil Online far beyond simple procedure. It encompasses that procedure but also the lodging of caveats and the case tracking of ordinary actions. One should not be surprised if in the next five years it becomes mandatory to use Civil Online for all litigation. At the present time the only paperwork that the sheriff clerk accepts initially is in relation to confirmation to estates of a deceased person (Forms C1, C5 and applications for eiks) and no doubt that will cease too.

Access to the system requires a password, each visit being controlled by the sending of a verification code sent to the user by email. This has to be entered by the user to unlock and gain access.

Civil Online also includes a facility for A.P.I. (application programming interface) whereby those undertaking the raising of cases in bulk can transfer data from their own case management systems to the court. This system was introduced in September 2021 and was updated in May 2023. It is aimed at the institutional client mentioned near the start of this book.

Interestingly, the compulsory use of Civil Online can be used as a tool to control the length of a party's submission to the court. Across all types of litigation there have been restrictions on the number of words in written pleadings. Assuming that the restriction is reasonable this is a perfectly legitimate policy. In early 2024 a party litigant in Ayr Sheriff Court submitted a 78-page set of submissions in an ordinary action. That smacks a little of over-enthusiasm.

There is no doubt that Civil Online has been a useful development for some, including institutional clients who litigate on an industrial scale and for whose solicitors the availability of A.P.I. has proved helpful in streamlining their debt recovery practices. It is also reflective of a process which is common throughout Commonwealth systems. For example, in Queensland, minor case claims, as they are known, must be submitted through the Electronic Case Management System.

On the other hand, and despite the option existing in exceptional cases, the removal of the availability of a paper submission option is unfortunate. S.C.T.S. promised that this choice would remain, but this appears to have been forgotten in the turmoil caused by Covid. The problem is that there is rampant discrimination in the court system against classes of citizen who do not qualify as possessing any of the protected characteristics as defined in the Equality legislation. So for example, the illiterate, semi-literate and now the computer illiterate are disadvantaged and vulnerable, as are those who do not have easy access to a computer, the elderly and those whose first language is not English. The author recalls observing a group of elderly homeless men being given assistance at Maryhill public library, Glasgow, in how to access benefits online. They were struggling. It seemed dogmatic and rather callous to insist that these individuals be compelled to use a system with which they were so uncomfortable.

Civil Online is a vehicle to online form completion and part of a drive towards electronic litigation. Ordinary Cause Rule 4A.2 directs that from 3rd July 2023 procedural business there is to be by electronic means unless in exceptional circumstances. Simple procedure may well follow.

CHAPTER FIVE

OTHER COMMONWEALTH SYSTEMS

In this book reference is made to small value practice and procedure in territories other than Scotland. In the context of a practical guide to Simple Procedure in Scotland it might at first blush seem irrelevant to consider other jurisdictions. However, consider the following;

1. Parochialism is unhelpful. Looking at other systems can help to illustrate features of our own, especially its shortcomings. We can usefully learn from how others deal with exactly the same types of disputes and factors that concern us here.

2. Simple procedure has been in existence for less than ten years. There is not yet enough reported caselaw in Scotland to allow a full analysis of all points. It might take many decades more before there is a sufficient body of reported cases.

3. Cases in Scotland are reported by S.C.T.S. and indeed in *Scots Law Times* and other such publications only if they involve a point of importance or complexity or novelty. The vast majority of simple procedure cases do not. Accordingly, they stay unreported. By contrast, the New Zealand authorities report numerous cases which would never be considered important enough to report here although they do concern the same types of issue that occur in simple procedure actions in Scotland. It is therefore illuminating to see how such cases are dealt with there.

The litigant who has a case involving a faulty washing machine has nothing with which to compare it. The position is different in New Zealand. It is worth looking at how proofs are conducted there under their Disputes Tribunal procedure;

https://www.disputestribunal.govt.nz/disputes-decision-finder/?Filter_Jurisdiction=26

A search for "washing machine" brings up nine cases, three of them from 2024. There are two on "double glazing" and twenty eight on "kitchen", eight of them from 2024. Nothing like this exists in Scotland.

Scotland and New Zealand have roughly the same population. Their systems for dealing with small value actions is different however, and that of New Zealand is better. There, small value cases are processed by a tribunal presided over by a referee. Scotland should adopt a similar approach, taking small value claims out of the sheriff court altogether. There are five main distinctions between the Scottish and New Zealand systems. In the latter;

1. Lawyers are not allowed to participate (as is the case in South Africa too). Incidentally, this used to be the case in Scotland two hundred years ago. Section 5 of the Justice of the Peace Small Debt (Scotland) Act 1825 prohibited legal representation.

2. Referees need not be legally qualified

3. Cases do not need to be decided strictly on legal obligations and duties

4. Cases are heard in private

5. Written judgments are issued which are easily accessible, short and comprehensible to laypersons.

These features may well jar in the mindset of a Scottish lawyer. However, assuming that the referees possess common sense, sound judgment and a sense of fairness (which a perusal of the reported cases indicates to be the case) the system appears to produce the correct results. As long as the outcomes are broadly fair the system is a success even if the routes to these results may seem unconventional and instinctively questionable to a

Scottish solicitor. It needs to be remembered that the courts, and indeed all forms of dispute resolution, are there to serve the people, not the legal profession.

None of these five factors listed above applies in simple procedure in the sheriff court. As a result, the description of that procedure as being inexpensive, speedy and informal all too often fails to materialise.

Nobody can seriously suggest that a dispute about a £35 dog collar (see below) is important enough to consume the time or cost either of a lawyer or a sheriff. There is also the question of over-qualification. Some summary sheriffs are senior counsel, accustomed to the Court of Session which does not hear payments actions worth less than £100,000.

In England too, the economics make little sense. There, small value claims are heard by district judges or circuit judges receiving an annual salary of £126,514 and £157,705 respectively.

A recent advertisement seeking referees for the New Zealand Tribunal stated that the remuneration was $NZ 530 per day, the equivalent of about £250 and that the hours are 8.30am to 5pm.

The third point above is an intriguing one. A cynic would interpret it as meaning that the law can be banished as an inconvenience. Others may see it as facilitating the application of plain common sense without the fetters of technical restraints. The New Zealand caselaw demonstrates the potential for the latter.

KN v XD Inc [2024] N.Z.D.T. 131 is a good example of the triumph of pragmatism over strict adherence to legal principles. The case concerned a missing pool cue. The pursuer sued for $660 for a new cue. The defender produced website evidence of secondhand cues selling for $20 to $130. The referee split the difference between $130 and $660 and granted an order for payment of $395 (about £180). He could have awarded $75, the middle ground between $20 and $130. However, given the paltry value of the action, on any ground, it is hardly worth spending the resources of a court in dealing with it.

A system which forbids solicitors and advocates from appearing is actually doing them a favour. The notion that simple procedure can be conducted by a solicitor informally is absurd. Lawyers do not do anything informally, nor should they. One would never expect a solicitor to draw up a will or buy a house informally. It would be interesting to see how a colleague would fare in a S.L.C.C. complaint by answering that she had been dealing with a court case informally.

CHAPTER SIX

THE MISNOMER THAT IS SIMPLE PROCEDURE

Labels and descriptions should never be taken at face value. A rose by any other name smells as sweet._A philosopher once observed that the Holy Roman Empire was in fact none of those things. Centuries later, part of that territory, known by then as the German Democratic Republic, was undemocratic. So is the Democratic Republic of Korea. An army does not become a more benign institution by naming it a "defence force". Closer to home is a principle of Scots law that description does not make something that which it is not. For example, a lease does not become a licence to occupy merely by describing it as such.

Simple procedure is often not simple. The name is more aspirational than correctly descriptive. This is not the first time that a system has claimed to promote rapidity; the Yorkshire Small Debts Recovery Act 1839 had the preamble that it was "An Act for the more easy and speedy recovery of small debts" in various parishes of that county.

This is not to say that everyone's experience of simple procedure will be challenging or complex, merely that the name is a misnomer. It would have been far better to have retained the name of the system which was replaced, Small Claims Procedure. True, a large part of summary cause procedure was replaced too but not all of it. No small claim has been raised since 2016. That name is freely available.

Small Claims Procedure has the qualities of being an accurate description and being akin to the name of low value action in many other English-speaking jurisdictions, including New South Wales, Northern Ireland, the Irish Republic, South Africa ("speedy, affordable and simple manner") and Ontario.

In addition, to compound the misdescription, when simple procedure was introduced in 2016 it was lauded by those who enacted it as being a speedy, inexpensive and informal way of resolving disputes. The problem is that such descriptions set expectations and when reality bites and these expectations are thwarted the litigant will feel disillusioned, disappointed and disgruntled. Too often, sluggishness, cost and the lack of an effective remedy become flies in the ointment.

The following three cases illustrate how value and simplicity are not correlates. The first two are reported on the S.C.T.S. website. The third never engendered any litigation.

Scottish Woodlands Ltd v Majekodunmi and another [2019] SAC (Civ) 38 was a claim for £405.60 in relation to an annual management charge by virtue of a real burden in the defenders' property title. Despite its small value there was nothing simple about it. Both sides appealed after the sheriff determined the case without hearing evidence. The appeal court was critical of that approach, held that the sheriff had erred and recalled the decision that had been reached. There was also criticism of the sheriff's having recorded that "the facts were agreed" when they were not. The appeal court commented that as regards a crucial figure "it might be unfair to say that the summary sheriff plucked it out of the air, as was suggested in submissions." and opined that "the claim as averred is so convoluted and lacking in specification as to be virtually meaningless." In any event, this case was devoid of simplicity.

In *Walkingshaw v Glenalmond Trading Industries Ltd* [2024] SC PER 47 which concerned the provision of a flowing screed, the judgment, dated 14th October 2024 extends to 144 pages, two witnesses were certified as skilled, counsel was instructed and the pursuer's agent was given a 30% uplift in fees. However, the sum eventually awarded was only £7120.85. That is not far above the simple procedure upper limit of £5000 and falls below the English equivalent of £10,000.

It is vital to identify the correct person to sue. This can be far from straightforward. Here is an example of a scenario that illustrates that a small value claim is not necessarily simple. Mercifully, this dispute was resolved before any action was raised.

The client attended an amateur dramatic production at a church hall. All proceeds went to charity. Her companion handed the client's coat and her own jacket to a boy in his early teens manning the cloakroom. A sign read "All garments are left at the owner's risk; no responsibility is accepted for any loss". At the end of the show the client went to retrieve the coat and jacket only to find that the coat was missing. The boy had been replaced by a lady in her seventies. The client obtained the coat in a sale at B.H.S. using a gift voucher given to her as a Christmas present two years before this theatrical mishap.

Lawyers would describe this kind of situation as being "like an exam question". All that is missing are two words at the end, namely "*Quid juris?*" or "What is the law?". Also, to complete the scene there would also probably be an implausible factor such as a winning lottery ticket languishing in one of the coat pockets.

On a practical level the client's wish was simple; she just wanted her coat back. But then the thorny questions arose;

1. Who ought she to sue? Her companion, the boy, the am dram society (under simple procedure it is permissible to sue an unincorporated association in its own name), the manager of the church hall, the church or the elderly lady. Or more than one of them.

2. Were any of them actually at fault?

3. Was the claim based on negligence or breach of contract?

4. What did anybody do that they ought not to have done?

5. What did any of them not do that they ought to have done? (and bear in mind that the client still does not actually know the fate of the coat or how it went missing or where it is now).

6. What was the legal effect, if any, of the disclaimer of liability notice?

7. Where is the coat now? Who last saw it?

Then hurdles become apparent;

a. The client did not know the name, let alone the address of the boy or the old lady.

b. She valued the friendship of her companion more than a coat.

c. She would feel heartless suing a schoolboy or an elderly lady, especially when they had given up their free time for a worthy cause.

d. The boy was quite possibly under 16, so she would have to involve his parents or guardians in the dispute.

e. The am dram society was an unincorporated association. So (probably) was the church. So, the client would have to sue office bearers and she had no idea of who they were.

f. Identifying the manager of the church hall was also problematic. It could be a committee, trustees, a limited or unlimited company, a partnership or a hybrid type of organisation.

There was a morass of problems before the Claim Form for delivery was even drafted. In fact, the scenario described never metamorphosised into a claim because the client agreed, very sensibly, not to pursue the matter after having received an apology from the church hall management, much to the relief of her agent.

Under simple procedure it is permissible to sue an unincorporated association in its own name. Generally, it is unwise to do this, particularly if the association is small, with no fixed address and with no obvious assets. Clubs, societies and the like can be ephemeral, here today and gone tomorrow. They can change their name, members and office bearers overnight. An association might be the Pittenweem Strolling Players one day and the East Neuk Thespians the next and their secretary might have changed from Olivia Bankhead to Austin Barraclough. Such evolutions can be informal, fluid, unrecorded and utterly infuriating. Such is the nature of unincorporated associations.

Having mentioned the perils of suing an unincorporated association it must be said that pursuing a case on behalf of such an entity is even more hazardous than suing one.

This is due to the fundamental problem that this type of body can melt away like snow in a thaw, a factor over which the solicitor has no control. The author had a disagreeable experience when he raised an ordinary action on behalf of an owners' association. To employ another analogy, in the initial stages all went well and everyone was happily on board. All was merry and bright. However, when the ship hit choppy waters they all grew squeamish, lost their nerve and began infighting and resigning. When the last man jumped overboard the association ceased to exist in the middle of the litigation and the case collapsed. This is a court lawyer's nightmare. There are two reasons; expenses and personal liability. By way of contrast, when an individual dies or becomes bankrupt or where an incorporated entity is wound up in the midst of a court action the claim transmits to a representative or successor such as an executor or trustee. In the case of an unincorporated association this does not happen. Instead, there is all too often a squabbling unseemly melee of individuals all vying to evade responsibility and leaving the lawyer in the lurch.

Worse, who pays the expenses of the abortive action? It is a fundamental tenet of Scots law of agency that the agent of a non-existent principal has personal liability. This is why a solicitor should, on purportedly being instructed by a limited company, check with Companies House that the company does indeed exist. It is worth checking the continuing position periodically.

On the next occasion where the author was instructed by an unincorporated association (a football supporters' club) to raise a court action he first ensured that there were signed mandates not just from the President, Secretary and Treasurer but from every member of the club, of which there were dozens.

Turning from the parties to the subject matter reveals the potential for further complexities.

Regard must always be had to the ineluctability of black letter law. This is the term given to the law as laid down in statutes and caselaw. Regardless of how simple the procedure governing a court action (any court action) if the black letter law is complicated the case will be so too. Two areas illustrate the point;

Consumer credit legislation is, to put it mildly, a challenging field to navigate. One suspects that the Consumer Credit Act 1974 has never been superseded because in the last fifty years nobody has had the stamina or stomach to tackle such a monumental task. The Act has spawned a gargantuan mass of secondary and subordinate legislation. Who amongst us has the strength of resolve to delve into this almost impenetrable warren to find the elusive answer to the client's query over whether she is entitled to return a faulty microwave oven that she acquired on hire purchase online?

Time bar is another key area of black letter law and one that affects every dispute. Many obligations become time barred after 5 years, under the Prescription and Limitation (Scotland) Act 1973. That Act it is not mentioned anywhere in the Simple Procedure Rules. It is *pars judicis* for the sheriff to notice points of time bar, although identifying whether or not an obligation has prescribed can sometimes be tricky.

Having discussed the issues above it is now proposed to look at the Simple Procedure Rules. It is re-iterated that although these are the most examined element of the law of simple procedure they must be treated as merely part of a much broader body of law governing this form of litigation. Also, please note the distinction between the Rules and the Regulations.

CHAPTER SEVEN

THE STRUCTURE OF THE SIMPLE PROCEDURE RULES

There has been a general drive towards encouraging litigation to be front loaded, meaning that the pursuer has to do a great deal of preparation and work at the early stages of the action as opposed to later. That burden is soon shared by the defender too. This is reflected in simple procedure although not as much as when the system was introduced; the Claims and the Response Forms 3A and 4A are both now less onerous to complete in that there is now no need to concern oneself with supplying witness details or lodging written evidence at that initial stage.

Traditionally, ordinary actions are not generally front loaded. As long as an Initial Writ contains the basics, such as a statement as to jurisdiction, it can be skeletal. For the solicitor entrusted with a claim which is about to become time barred the imperative is to get a writ drafted, warranted and served by sheriff officer as soon as possible. As long as that can be achieved it does not matter if the writ is bare, inelegant or lacking detail; these deficiencies can all be cured by expanding it later by adjustment. There is no point in going to the effort of drafting and then refining and polishing a writ if the claim prescribes before it is served.

Certainly, there are exceptions. Firstly, the court rules sometimes require that a writ contain certain averments. So an action for parental orders must say that there are no orders in existence under the Adoption Act. Also, the Ordinary Cause Rules include requirements to lodge certain documents with a writ at the stage of having it warranted for service. The sheriff clerk will not warrant a divorce writ unless it is accompanied by an extract marriage certificate. There is a distinct, discrete set of rules governing personal injury claims in the ordinary court. These actions are far more front loaded than other types of ordinary cause, with far more emphasis on disclosure of evidence, obviously designed to facilitate settlement. This also seems to be a feature of simple procedure.

Small claims procedure was not front loaded. It did not have to be because if the action were defended there was a preliminary hearing which took place in open court, and the issues were supposed to be aired and discussed at that diet.

By contrast, as we will see later, there is no preliminary hearing in a simple procedure case. The sheriff is specifically directed to consider the Claim Form and Response Form in private (see below). The court has the power under 1.8 to grant a decree (or "decision") or to dismiss an action without even giving the parties a chance to make representations.

The claimant has to clear two early hurdles; a) that at which the action is warranted by the sheriff clerk, and b) the 7.5 exercise by the sheriff in chambers of deciding how a defended case is to progress. There could then be c) a case management discussion (the nearest equivalent of the small claim preliminary hearing) fixed in terms of 7.6.

The sheriff has wide powers to dispose of the case without having heard a single witness. Leaving aside these hazards of a case being dismissed or decree granted the shrieval scrutiny required by the rules will not be effective and the whole system will not work as it should unless the material provided to the court by the claimant and respondent is considerably more than would have been lodged initially by the pursuer of a small claim.

Structurally, the rules are inferior to the Small Claims Rules 2002. Essentially, they are constructed as a set of questions and answers. There is really no need for this.

The Simple Procedure Rules refer to chapters as "Parts" adopting the terminology used in the Civil Practice Rules of England and Wales. In that jurisdiction, incidentally, low value claims are heard in the County

Court and the procedure is governed by C.P.R. Part 27, named "The Small Claims Track" and there is also a Practice Direction 27A.

The Simple Procedure Rules repeatedly fail to prioritise the practical issues of litigation. The enormously complex and vital topic of expenses is reduced to a Part consisting of twenty-four lines including six questions the most pointless of which has to be "What is this Part about?". This is followed by the equally facile but also garbled answer "This Part is about the expenses of a claim which the sheriff can order a party to pay for".

By contrast, there are thirty lines devoted to references to the European Court of Justice of the European Union, and interventions by the Commission for Equality and Human Rights and the Scottish Commission for Human Rights. From the author's own observations and research such references and interventions are about as common as a proof that actually starts at 10am.

CHAPTER EIGHT

PRINCIPLES, POWERS AND THE DEFINITION OF A SIMPLE PROCEDURE CLAIM

Part 1 is described as **An overview of simple procedure.** It consists of eight questions, 1.1 to 1.8, to which there are fifty-eight answers some of which can be regarded as rules and other simply statements. Some of them are worthless. 1.1 asks "What is simple procedure?", and the answer is then given that it "is a court process designed to provide a speedy, inexpensive and informal way to resolve disputes."

1.2 deals with "the principles of simple procedure." It was analysed by the Sheriff Appeal Court in the one appeal comprising three cases *Cabot Financial UK Ltd v Robert McGregor, Liam Gardner and Kirsty Brown* [2018] SAC (Civ) 12

That judgment is probably the most useful so far on how simple procedure is supposed to operate. In particular, it clarifies that sheriffs are not meant to embark upon enquiries into the merits of undefended action, but must adhere to the standard topics of jurisdiction, time bar and competency which are common to any court action.

Where the case is less helpful is in relation to the 1.2 principles. It clarified that these are not rules but are objectives intended to change the ethos of how the "litigation is conducted, underpinning the exercise of the court's case management powers."(p25)

This sounds very commendable but, with the exception of the second one, none of the five principles in 1.2 is innovative or remarkable at all. These are the principles;

1. Cases are to be resolved as quickly as possible, at the least expense to parties and the courts.

The desire to achieve time and cost efficiencies is as old as the hills, and the task of doing so has always proved Sisyphean. Since Dickens wrote of the Jarndyce case in *Bleak House* (1853) the mischiefs of delay and costs have been well known to the public.

2. The approach of the court to a case is to be as informal as is appropriate, taking into account the nature and complexity of the dispute.

This injunction to be informal is ambiguous. It could mean that the sheriff is to address the litigants using their first names, as has happened in Child Welfare Hearings in Glasgow, or is allowed to use profane language, as has also happened in such hearings. It could permit lawyers to appear wearing jeans, trainers and an open collar shirt, as occurred during Covid restrictions, or to drink coffee and eat chocolates in court, as the author once observed happening in Lanark sheriff court. On the other hand, does this call for informality extend to adherence to rules such as time limits or to proving formal service? (see *Cabot Financial UK Ltd v Ryan Bell* 2023 CSIH 43) From the perspective of solicitors, it is dangerous to act informally in conducting any litigation.

Courts are not really supposed to be informal places. Few members of the public would expect them to be, and many are likely to be confused if they arrive at a court building to find that the judge is indistinguishable in attire and manner from the garrulous fellow serving tea and biscuits to raise funds for good causes at the mobile servery in the corridor outside the courtroom.

3. Parties are to be treated even-handedly by the court.

This statement of the obvious really ought not to be taking up space within the Simple Procedure

Rules. It smacks of an attempt to re-assure party litigants that there will be equality of arms even if their opponents are represented by senior counsel.

It is important to note that there are limits to how far a court in Scotland or anywhere else can legitimately go in assisting unrepresented parties. In *Khaliq v Gutowski 2019 SC 136* the Inner House stated that the court is not to act as adviser to a party litigant (in relation to grounds of appeal). Although a party litigant can be helped to understand proceedings generally, a court cannot assist him to win his case; *Barton v Wright Hassall* LLP [2018] UKSC 12. This authority was referred to by the Sheriff Appeal Court in *Doran V SC Causewayside Ltd* [2023] SAC (Civ) 10 where the court held that "The appellant demands too much of the sheriff and too little of himself."

4. Parties are to be encouraged to settle their disputes by negotiation or alternative dispute resolution and should be able to do so throughout the progress of a case.

There has never been a court in which the sheriff would not have preferred that the litigants settle the case extra-judicially. It is human nature to try to avoid making important decisions that affect other people, especially if one of those persons will be cross or upset. This is why a sheriff will have to conceal her glee when a proof has to be discharged due to lack of court time. The application of this principle expressing the desire for settlement "throughout the progress of a case" has been tested in connection with the lodging of a Tender; *Jamie Davis v Skyfire Insurance* [2019] SC EDIN 24 (of which more later).

5. Parties should only have to come to court when it is necessary to do so to progress or resolve their dispute.

This is another platitude. It has always been standard practice for a writ to include the statement

"This action is necessary". Anyone who raises an action needlessly is likely to find not just that he fails to obtain an award of expenses but that he is found liable to the defender in some of the expenses.

1.3 enquires "Who takes part?" and then refers to the *dramatis personae* as being sheriff, parties, representatives and the sheriff clerk. It does not mention courtroom supporters (see Part 2 below). Then, 1.4 to 1.8 deal with the responsibilities of those parties respectively.

Lastly, after the topic of responsibilities has been exhausted, 1.8 concerns the sheriff's powers.

This Part of the rules was amended by Act of Sederunt twice, in 2016 and 2023 but only in minor ways; it is largely as it was when first introduced. From a practical perspective of a solicitor the most important of these provisions is 1.8.

1.8 (3) is the widest of powers, enabling the sheriff to "do anything or give any order considered necessary to decide the case." This subsumes others such as that in terms of 1.8(9) whereby the "sheriff may pause and restart" the case. 1.8(4) is the court's dispensing power. That power was in Small Claim Rule 3.1.(1) but it need not specifically be included anywhere in the Simple Procedure Rules. Standing 1.8(3) it does not have to be.

Part 1 is actually so over-simplified as to be useless in fundamental ways. In the spirit of endeavouring to be simple let us take a straightforward question, one which is not included in Part 1 but which ought to be;

<u>What is the definition of a simple procedure claim?</u>

Broadly (see question below), any claim for payment of £5000 or less, or any *action ad factum praestandum* or for delivery of moveables where there is an alternative crave for £5000 or less must be brought as a simple procedure action. If there is no such alternative crave it is incompetent to bring the action under simple procedure; *Black Horse Ltd v Cameron*

[2019] SC DUM 36, 2019 SLT (Sh Ct) 155. In addition, one has to have regard to whether there are any statutory provisions excluding the sheriff's jurisdiction. Section 16 of the Housing (Scotland) Act 2014 transfers to the First-tier Tribunal that power in relation to actions arising from private tenancies. If, for example, a tenant blocked a toilet with cat litter a claim seeking reimbursement of the plumber's bill could not be by simple procedure. The statutory remedy of compensation for unfair dismissal claims – as opposed to wrongful dismissal – must be pursued before the Employment Tribunal. On the other hand, there is nothing to prevent a cohabitant's claim for a capital sum under the Family Law (Scotland) Act 2006 from being by simple procedure.

The upper limit of £5000 has never been raised. That sum in 2016 is worth almost £7000 in 2024 and should be increased accordingly.

Another question that must be asked is whether there are any types of payment action for less than £5000 that cannot be brought under simple procedure. Assume that a very unfortunate client has been the target of a libellous post on social media, she has seen the message on her phone whilst shopping in a supermarket and has then left angrily and hurriedly, slipping on the wet floor and sustained minor bruising. Can she sue the defamer and the occupier of the shop respectively?

The answer to both is in the negative but one would never know that from even a careful perusal of the Simple Procedure Rules. Instead, to reach that conclusion requires that we travel down a complicated and meandering path due to legislation which, on the face of it, has nothing to do with simple procedure;

Simple procedure was activated on 28th November 2016 by the Courts Reform (Scotland) Act 2014 (Commencement No 7, Transitional and Savings Provisions) Order 2016. However, Rule 1 of that Order applies the procedure only to that which is described as a "relevant claim". Relevant claim is defined in the Order as being a claim brought after 28th November 2016 which

(a) would have been a Small Claim had there not been a repeal of those provisions of the Sheriff Courts (Scotland) Act 1971 which created Small Claims procedure, and

(b) on the assumption that the upper value limit is £5000 rather than £3000 (which was the upper limit of small claims in 2016).

Under those 1971 Act provisions there was secondary legislation, the Small Claims (Scotland) Order 1988, in which the definition of a Small Claim excluded actions of aliment, interim aliment and defamation. Then, the Small Claims (Scotland) Amendment Order 2007 amended the 1988 Order so as to add "and actions for personal injury", which removed personal injury from small claims procedure in 2008.

In other words, because by 2016 it was incompetent to raise a small claim action for aliment, defamation or personal injury it is equally incompetent to raise any of those actions under simple procedure. These types of action have to be raised under summary cause procedure, just as before 2016. True, section 74 of the 2014 Act permits aliment actions to be brought under simple procedure. However, that section is omitted from the 2016 Commencement Order and it has never been brought into force.

On the topic of law not having been brought into force it is worth remembering that it was intended, and probably still is, that actions of multiplepoinding, furthcoming and count, reckoning and payment would be competent under simple procedure. Instead, they still have to be brought under the Summary Cause Rules 2002 Chapters 27, 28 and 29 respectively. This is so regardless of their value. So in an estate worth a couple of thousand pounds, an argument between squabbling relatives claiming ownership of an album of family photographs or a residuary beneficiary demanding an accounting from the executor would have to be resolved by summary cause procedure. The author gave a talk to the Glasgow Bar Association in 2016, a month before the Simple Procedure Rules came into force, and advised, on the basis of the information then available, that Special Simple Procedure Rules governing these three remedies appeared likely to be brought in by around 2018. That was the prevailing view at the time. Some felt that there should in fact be one set of simple procedure rules governing all and every type of action worth £5000 or under. It is remarkable that summary cause procedure still remains, and that these three remedies have not been transferred to simple procedure with registered social housing evictions being placed under the jurisdiction of the First Tier Tribunal (Property and Housing Chamber) and Tenancy of Shops (Scotland) Act 1949 cases becoming summary applications.

CHAPTER NINE

REPRESENTATION AND SUPPORT

Part 2 consists of six questions, to which there are twenty-four answers. Some can be regarded as directions and other simply as statements. Importantly, this Part of the rules draws distinctions between representatives (of which there are two types, namely legal and lay); 2.2 to 2.4, and courtroom supporters; 2.5 and 2.6. This difference is reflected in the heading of Part 2, and this is a good thing. There is much scope for the involvement of individuals and it is important that they appreciate and respect the limits of their roles.

This Part of the Rules was amended by Act of Sederunt twice, in 2016 and 2018 but only slightly. The most significant amendment was to state that a trainee solicitor may be a legal representative. Under small claims procedure the rights of audience of trainee solicitors was a rather opaque topic. In Glasgow, certainly in the early days of the procedure, a firm would seek and obtain the approval of the sheriff principal (who at that time was Norman Macleod Q.C.) and the trainee could then appear, but not in proofs. Also, this limited authority was given only to second year trainees who obviously held a restricted practising certificate.

Now, first year trainees may appear, and there is nothing to prevent them conducting all diets, including proofs (or, in simple procedure parlance, hearings). Whether that is wise, however, is another matter and one that needs to be carefully considered by the supervising solicitor.

The Admission as Solicitor (Scotland) Regulations 2019 state at 1(2) of Schedule 3 that a trainee not admitted "may appear in the Sheriff Court in a Simple Procedure matter." Note though that if a firm of solicitors chooses to use a trainee to attend court a lower standard of care does not apply than if a qualified solicitor were used; *Dunhill v W Brook and Co* [2016] EWHC 165 (Q.B.)

As has been suggested already, solicitors should try to avoid appearing in simple procedure cases. The system is geared to try to discourage that from happening. That is the case here and also in other countries, due to restrictions or by outright prohibitions. One feels that lawyers are not made to feel welcome. Courts have not always seen them as having a benevolent influence. Sheriff Sir Walter Scott had strong views, and opined that there was "something sickening in seeing poor devils drawn into great expenses about trifles by interested attorneys."

In making the distinction between representatives and supporters Part 2 is clearer than the equivalent chapter in the Summary Cause Rules; in the latter, Chapter 2 is headed "Representation" but then has two rules, 2.1 governing representatives and 2.2 dealing with lay supporters. The latter should not be classified under that chapter heading, or the heading should be amended to make it clear that supporters are not representatives. Part 2 is an improvement in this regard. Summary Cause Rule 2A deals with "Lay Representation" specifically.

To appreciate the difference between representatives and supporters it is useful to consider the law of agency. Lay representatives are agents whereas supporters are not. However, that begs another question; what is the ostensible authority of a lay representative? This has practical consequences. It is well settled law that solicitors have ostensible authority to compromise an action (*Mazur v Primrose and Gordon [2015] CSIH 8*). In other words, if a lawyer offers £4000 in full and final settlement and the offer is accepted the lawyer's client is contractually bound to pay £4000 even if he did not in fact authorise the offer. Indeed, he need not even know about it. As to whether a lay representative has similar authority the answer is that it is very unlikely. Certainly, it would be unwise to rely on an offer made by a representative without making certain that the principal authorised it, preferably by signing a Joint Minute to that effect. Another difference between lawyers and lay representatives is that the latter are not officers of court, they are not insured, they have no professional standards to meet or code of conduct to follow and they cannot be the subject of a complaint to the S.L.C.C. These deficiencies, which are detrimental to the interests of litigants represented by lay people, are presumably why 1.6 exists. It is headed "What are representatives' responsibilities?" and applies to both legal and lay representatives. No doubt this is well meant but as regards the former it is unnecessary and in respect of the latter it is practically unenforceable. It includes such strictures as that "Representatives must maintain client confidentiality". Firstly, lay representatives have principals, not clients and, secondly, how can such an obligation actually be implemented against them short of the drastic step of a contempt of court finding? 1.6 purports to impose a code of conduct on unqualified representatives without there being any professional or disciplinary body to police it. This false equivalence of legal and lay representatives is potentially misleading litigants, who will believe that they are far better protected than they really are. For a good example of the problems that can arise where a litigant is represented by an unqualified person see the quasi-professional negligence case of *Paul Whyte v Troy Lucas (a firm) and George Rusz* [2019] EWHC 1098 QB.

As discussed, Part 1 deals with representatives' responsibilities but it does not mention courtroom supporters. These individuals are colloquially known as "McKenzie Friends" another English term to have permeated Scottish procedure. The examples given in the Rules are family members, friends or colleagues although there is no prohibition on anyone else being a supporter. 2.5(3) makes it explicit that a courtroom supporter may not receive any remuneration. By contrast, in England and Wales such persons are not precluded from being paid.

Courtroom supporters are expressly permitted in the Court of Session (RCS 12A.1.) and they are a feature of other court systems in Commonwealth countries too. In a sense, their legal status is clearer than those of lay representatives, not least because they are not agents and they have no authority to address the court. In the sheriff court there have always been courtroom supporters, but they were known to us as "the pursuer's mother" or similar. Putting them on a formal footing in the Scottish courts seems largely unnecessary.

CHAPTER TEN

SERVICE OF DOCUMENTS

Part 6 is headed **Sending and formal Service** and comprises 6.1 to 6.13 consisting of thirteen questions to which there are then twenty-nine broad answers. As in previous Parts, some can be regarded as rules, others as statements to guide and inform. This Part refers to Parts 18 and 19 which deal with formal service within and outwith Scotland respectively.

It is unclear why the reader has to jump a dozen Parts to reach these provisions. Sequentially, it would have made more sense to insert them immediately after Part 6. It would have been clearer to have had the method of witness citation included in Part 11 ("Witnesses") than here.

Part 6 concerns situations where "these Rules require something to be *sent* to someone" or, by contrast, where they "require a document to be formally *served* on someone." (italics added). So in terms of 11.2 a Witness List need only be sent whereas each witness citation (Witness Citation Notice") requires to be "formally served".

The use of the adjective "formal" here is pointless. There is nothing in the Rules about "informal service" (which would be a peculiar concept) so it would be better simply to use the term "service". The Small Claims Rules referred to service, delivery and intimation but not to "sending".

Taking the Simple Procedure Rules *verbatim* the crucial difference between sending and formally serving lies in who can undertake the exercise; the former may be done by anybody whereas the latter may be done only by the sheriff clerk, a solicitor or a sheriff officer. All three of these are officers of the court. There are public policy reasons that lie behind this. For all that there is a stated desire to make simple procedure a user-friendly system in which lawyers are redundant, everyone knows that giving party litigants *carte blanche* to cite witnesses is extremely unwise. Some individuals can be over-enthusiastic. Without some control there is the potential for an excess of zeal. A dozen individuals might be cited where only two are necessary. Citations might go to the Prime Minister, CEOs of social media companies and heads of state of foreign countries, this last category being non-compellable. This would bring the whole system into disrepute. Unless one were prepared for irresponsible citations being sent it is necessary to restrict the ability of litigants to carry out formal service.

There is another public policy factor too. People are more likely to obey a citation if they know that they will not be out of pocket by doing so. So, the solicitor is in effect compelled to underwrite the reimbursement of the costs incurred by a witness. This is why there is a rule that a solicitor who cites a witness is personally liable for his expenses. Ordinary Cause Rule 29.7(5) makes this explicit in relation to that form of procedure. This is not to say that the client is not personally liable too, but the person cited is far more likely to look to the lawyer for costs; she can be threatened with a complaint and she has insurance.

Under Summary Cause procedure this safeguard remains; there is also a rule, 18.9, headed "Citation of witnesses by party litigants" which requires such litigants to find caution to cover the expenses before instructing a solicitor or sheriff officer to cite. There was an identical rule under the 2002 Small Claims Rules, 17.5, but this measure has not made its way into the Simple Procedure Rules. So lawyers who agree to cite are more exposed than ever. Care is required.

6.3 concerns timing. It deals with when service has to be made. It states that where service has to be by a deadline it must arrive by the end of that period or day. If the end falls on a Saturday, Sunday, public holiday or court holiday (each of which is a *dies non,* meaning a "non-day") it is delayed until after that *dies non* has expired. Of course, a debate on the intricacies of the exact point at which a time limit expires can easily be avoided just by serving the document in plenty of time. Lawyers can have an unfortunate tendency to procrastinate until there is real urgency. The author is as guilty of this as anyone, having once started preparation at

4am for a proof due to commence six hours later. The requirement to act *by* a date should not be interpreted as waiting *until* the date before acting. On numerous occasions arguments have had to be made in court as to the exact time when a deadline expires, whether than be when the sheriff clerk's office shuts (which is usually early on a Friday), 5pm or midnight. The job is difficult and stressful enough without getting into these types of wrangle. Avoid them by acting early.

6.4 provides that a party who responds may not object to how that document was sent or formally served. This rule is applied widely throughout the courts and is to the effect that reacting to something irregularly served waives one's right to make an issue of the irregularity. Sometimes a recipient can be faced with a dilemma. Suppose Allan Baker receives a document addressed to Alan Barker, Allan Barker or Alan Baker. If he reacts, such as by lodging a Response Form, the spelling error or errors are rendered irrelevant as a defence to the proceedings. Essentially, he cures the defect. However, if he declines to react the result could be a decree or decision against a non-existent Allan Barker designed as residing at Allan Baker's address. That could lead to diligence following against Allan Baker. This type of muddle could also arise in relation to the mis-spelling of the name of a limited company.

6.5 concerns the "sending" (as opposed to the service) of documents. It does not require an officer of court for a document to be sent. It is important to check the options, because these depend on the scenario. 6.5 to 6.7 envisage three;

a) The court sending something to a party

b) The party sending something to the court.

c) The party sending something to another party.

There are five permissible methods but the choice is widest for a) and narrowest for c). Both delivery to a Document Exchange and the use of the S.C.T.S. Portal – through its website – are competent in a), b) and c), although it is unlikely that a party litigant will be a member of such an exchange.

Posting is competent in all three scenarios although in a) normal post is enough, in b) it needs to be by recorded delivery and in c) it must be recorded and also next day delivery. Accordingly, only the court may use the least onerous form of post.

Email may be used in a) and c) only

Handing over a document is permissible in a) and b) only. The use of the former is likely to be a rare occurrence. It would require that the party is physically in the court building, perhaps in the sheriff clerk's office.

Internet interface may be used to send a Claim Form to the court in b) only. This is to enable the use of Civil Online.

Sheriff officers may be used in relation to c) if other methods have failed. So, unusually for them, they would be sending rather than serving.

6.8 governs formal service on someone domiciled in Scotland; a direction is made to the terms of Part 18. This Part is considered later.

6.9 governs formal service on someone domiciled outwith Scotland, and a direction is made to the terms of Part 19. This Part is also considered later. Every country in the world can be allocated to one of the categories described in that Part and these set out the available means of service. Depending on the location of the respondent these means may involve more hope than expectation of success.

6.11 concerns formal service of the Claim Form 3A on the respondent. This is a crucial step, since it denotes the commencement of an action (*Alston v Macdougall* (1887) 15 R 78.). For the purposes of avoiding time bar and a negligence claim, this needs attention.

6.12 applies where the address of the respondent is unknown. There is only one method of service prescribed, namely advertisement on the

S.C.T.S. website. There is a Form 6B headed "Service by Advertisement Application".

Clicking on "Courts and Tribunals" takes the reader to another heading "General Public Notices" The list of all cases where the respondent's whereabouts are unknown is displayed here, including simple procedure cases along with bankruptcy petitions, ordinary actions and the like.

Until recently, two rather antiquated methods were available, namely display on the walls of court and advertisement in a newspaper. These are still referred to in the Ordinary Cause Rules (O.C.R. 5.6) even although walls of court service is treated by the sheriff clerk as being on the S.C.T.S. website and not a physical wall. By contrast, the Simple Procedure Rules reflect actual practice.

Both these means of service were largely hollow exercises. The former was particularly futile, predicated on the fanciful notion that a defender would happen to be wandering past the sheriff clerk's notice board whereupon amongst the papers festooning it he would serendipitously observe a copy of a document directed at himself. The latter method of service was marginally less a token exercise. It sometimes led to the sheriff having to assess which publication a defender was likely to read. Various assumptions or prejudices would come into play, such that a stockbroker last seen in Stockbridge would read a broadsheet whereas a milkman from Castlemilk was likely to be a tabloid reader. Neither of these stereotypes is likely to be reading the S.C.T.S Website for entertainment or any other reason, however.

Practitioners would always try to persuade the sheriff to opt for walls of court service rather than newspaper service to avoiding the expense of paying the advertising cost.

6.13 is where the sheriff is not satisfied that formal service has been made. Essentially, he can require re-service.

Part 18 is headed **Formal Service in Scotland** This Part is short, comprising 18.1 to 18.3

As we have seen, reference has already been made to 6.8, which governs formal service on someone domiciled in Scotland; one is directed to the terms of Part 18. It is unclear why this and Part 19, both of which relate to service, are located towards the end of the Rules.

In ordinary cause procedure a plea of "No jurisdiction" can be fatal, although far more commonly the sheriff will transfer the cause to the correct court rather than dismissing it. This can only be on the motion of a party, though, and only if the sheriff considers it expedient to do so, which can only be if there are other factors. It is hard to envisage when it would not be expedient; there seems to be very little point in wasting time and resources by dismissing a case erroneously raised in Glasgow sheriff court rather than Hamilton due to confusion over the jurisdictional status of a street in Rutherglen, through which runs the frontier between the two sheriffdoms. The dispute will simply be litigated again, delaying its resolution.

Jurisdiction and domicile are not words that one will find in simple procedure. That forum tries to avoid the problems that can arise from someone suing in the incorrect sheriff court by creating a mechanism for the transfer to the correct one *ex proprio motu*.

Small claim rule 15.1(2) did this too, stating that the sheriff "may" transfer the cause. Summary Cause Rule 16(1)(2) still does this. Simple procedure is stronger. Although it is classified as one of the sheriff's powers rather than responsibilities, 1.8(17) provides that where a case has been raised in the wrong court the sheriff "must" transfer it to the correct court "unless ... there is a good reason not to". This makes sense. In any event, territorial boundaries are becoming increasing irrelevant as litigation migrates online. In effect a Webex hearing takes place in the parties' homes or offices regardless of the location stipulated at the top of the writ.

18.1 announces that "This Part is about how to formally serve a document on someone living in Scotland." This means a person domiciled there.

18.2 states that where the Rules require formal service "the first attempt must be by"

(a) "a next-day postal service which records delivery", or

(b) email if the intended recipient "has indicated a willingness to accept service" by that method, which "may be expressed specifically to the claimant or generally (for example on a website)"

Such service may be undertaken only by the party's solicitor or a sheriff officer. In addition, where the claimant is not a company, limited liability partnership or partnership and the claimant is not legally represented 6.11(2) empowers the sheriff clerk to serve the Claim Form; no mention is made of any other documents, however.

There are three points that can be made here;

Firstly, 18.2 requires that postal or email service be used before sheriff officers may be instructed. This is an innovation and one which makes little sense. By contrast, the Small Claims Rules 2002 contained no equivalent restriction. The respondent might be a recalcitrant who has never shown any willingness to accept email service of court documents and who has no intention of answering the door to the postman. Sheriff officer service will inevitably be necessary and there is no point in wasting time and energy meantime on a futile attempt at postal service.

Secondly, a claim might be about to become time barred imminently. Service needs to be swift and reliable, which necessitates instructing sheriff officer service. The alternative methods are too risky.

Thirdly, to deter the needless deployment of sheriff officer service there is an appropriate sanction, that being to refuse to allow the claimant to recover this outlay in the event that she wins the case and is awarded expenses. That is the practice in ordinary procedure. It ought to be the same here too.

Solicitors, sheriff officers and the sheriff clerk are all officers of the court. Restricting to them the right to serve documents formally recognises the importance of the task.

18.2(3) requires that the service envelope bears a direction that if service cannot be made the papers are to be returned immediately to the sheriff clerk. This is a long standing and standard practice across all forms of litigation in the courts, intended to alert the court speedily that postal service has failed. It also alerts the intended recipient, of course, that the envelope is likely to contain unfriendly contents.

18.2(4) provides that where there has been formal service "a Confirmation of Formal Service must be completed and any evidence of sending or, in the case of email, proof of receipt attached to it." This form, known as Form 6C, has caused a plethora of litigation despite its seemingly being so innocuous. It was used in connection with service of a claim using proof of sending rather than proof of receipt in the case of *Ryan Bell* (already referred to in relation to 1.2.) The sheriff held that this was adequate, having regard to *Cabot Financial UK Ltd v Finnegan* 2021 SLT (Sh Ct) 237 *and Cabot Financial UK Ltd v Donnelly* 2022 SLT (Sh Ct) 147. However, when the case was appealed the Sheriff Appeal Court held that this was wrong and that evidence of delivery needed to be produced. On further appeal to the Inner House the decision of the Sheriff Appeal Court was overturned and the sheriff's determination was reinstated, the Lord President referring to the "long-established presumption, proof of sending is proof of delivery."

18.3 "What if service by post does not work?" governs sheriff officer service. It does not mention the Fees of Messengers-at-Arms and Sheriff

Officers (Amendment) S.S.I. 2024 No.41, which determines the cost of this exercise.

Part 19 is headed **Formal Service Outside Scotland** and consists of 19.1 to 19.7.

Since this is a practical guide it is worth repeating that those who have to embark upon serving a Claim Form on overseas debtors are probably on a fool's errand or wild goose chase with only a worthless decree and a lawyer's bill to show at the end of it.

Clients need to be warned about the likely futility of pursuing money owed by anybody located in just about any part of the world outwith the United Kingdom. It can be hard advising a client in Scotland that it was naïve to sell and deliver goods to a customer in Abu Dhabi or Zambia without payment, insurance or guarantors here, but far harder by the time that he has spent more than the cost of the goods in funding a pursuit of a debtor over the hills and far away halfway across the globe.

Reference has been made above to 6.9, which deals with formal service on someone domiciled outwith Scotland. It directs the reader to the terms of Part 19. Every part of the planet falls into one of the categories below. These determine the available means of service. Some are more reliable than others depending on conditions on the ground. For example, a quarter of the world's population lives in areas affected by conflict, according to the United Nations. A claim from Scotland for a few thousand pounds is hardly likely to be a priority.

Anyone contemplating suing a respondent beyond the borders of Scotland ought to be mindful of broader economic realities too. Obtaining a Scottish decree is not really the problem. It is quite conceivable that nobody will bother defending the claim. Enforcing it is a different matter entirely even in politically stable countries. It is challenging enough to do so even in Scotland. A bird in the hand is worth two in the bush, especially one growing in the harsh terrain of Morocco or Pakistan. In their hearts, clients will probably know that an action against, for example, a vendor in Taiwan is likely to be a money pit yielding nothing but tears, but lawyers need to be able to vouch that they have advised accordingly.

Of course, practitioners here are not qualified in foreign law or insured to advise upon it, but we all instinctively know that unless in exceptional circumstances, for a debt of no more than £5000 most clients will be well advised to take it put it down to experience rather than throwing good money after bad in trying to recover it from a foreign debtor.

Unremarkably, there is nothing in the Rules about enforcing a simple procedure outwith Scotland. The position is far too complicated and collating the procedures would be a task of the magnitude of compiling the Domesday Book. Also, it would take an army of researchers and scribes to maintain such a work. Part 15 "How to enforce a decision." relates to Scotland only.

For service in Scotland the costs are known or, at least, they can be reasonably easily estimated. Sheriff officer fees are regulated by the Act of Sederunt (Fees of Messengers at Arms and Sheriff Officers) (Amendment) 2024, the most recent of a succession of measures updating the Act of Sederunt of 2002. By contrast, the cost of engaging process servers in Nigeria or elsewhere is a topic well beyond the scope of this book.

In addition, in relation to service overseas there are the expenses of engaging the services of a translator if the defender is not in an Anglophone country (which includes most countries).

For the brave or foolhardy, Part 19 explains how to serve the Claim Form abroad. The Part is lengthy, comprising over two hundred lines.

In addition, it appears to be out of date. Regulation (EC) No 1393/2007 on the service of judicial and extrajudicial documents in civil or commercial matters once used to regulate the position between the UK and the other European Union member states. However, as of 31st

December 2020 it ceased to apply, leaving the Hague Service Convention on service of commercial and civil documents, 15th November 1965, as the governing measure. All 27 of the EU members states are signatories to that Hague Convention. Accordingly, the position is now the same as between Austria and Australia, Peru and Peruglia.

In terms of Part 19 countries and territories are divided into five categories. International service is complicated because the U.K. is divided into several distinct jurisdictions of which Scotland is one. The five classifications as are follows;

19.3 England, Wales, Northern Ireland (i.e the rest of the United Kingdom) plus the Isle of Man and the Channel Islands.

This is the easiest category, not least because all the others are complicated due to language barriers. Recorded delivery post may be used. Or, personal service may be made by someone who is entitled to serve documents under the domestic law of that territory. 19.3(4) is analogous to 6.11(2) (service of the Claim Form by the sheriff clerk) and 19.3(7) to 18.3. (the label on the service envelope) These provisions also apply *mutatis mutandis* in relation to service in the other categories of state, noted below. If the country is not Anglophone there will have to be two labels, one in English and the other in the language of the country concerned

19.4 A member state of the European Union

19.4 asks "How can you formally serve a document on someone who lives in an EU member state ... under the Service Regulation?"

"Service Regulation" is defined in Regulation 3 (the interpretation regulation) as meaning Regulation (EC) No 1393/2007 already mentioned. It is obsolete. 19.4 should be revoked. Meantime, practitioners should disregard it and treat E.U states under 19.5.

Quantum valeat, 19.4 prescribes 4 possible methods of service, "depending on what the law of that member state permits". These are;

a. "Postal service", i.e. recorded delivery post

b. "Service by transmitting agency", which is giving the papers to a messenger at arms (not a mere sheriff officer). 19.4(9) and (10) require that the messenger be given a translation of the document in a language that the recipient will understand or of the official language of that country. There also needs to be a Translation Certificate from the interpreter to say that the foreign language version is a correct translation of the English one. Suing a Belgian respondent would require the applicant to assess whether the appropriate translation should be French or Flemish. One or other would suffice even if the recipient is an asylum seeker who understands only Somali.

c. "Direct service", i.e. giving the papers to someone entitled to serve documents in that territory.

d. "Consular service", which entails asking the Foreign and Commonwealth Office to serve. "This method can always be used" if the recipient is a British national.

The caveat of "depending on what the law of that member state permits" creates something of a conundrum. The law of Scotland is deemed to be within the judicial knowledge of the sheriff. The domestic law of other countries is not, although there is a (rather shaky) presumption that foreign law complies with Scots law. This begs the question of how the Scottish court can be satisfied that, for example, the law of Cyprus allows service by local courier of a simple procedure Claim Form on a respondent in Larnaca.

19.5 <u>A state which is a member of the Hague Service Convention on service of commercial and civil documents, 15th November 1965, (other than one which is also a EU member state)</u>

Post Brexit, the words in brackets are redundant.

A surprisingly large number of countries are not members. In Africa, for example, only Eqypt, Tunisia, Morocco (including Western Sahara), Malawi and Botswana are members. In the Middle East only Israel and Kuwait are members

The rules prescribe 4 possible methods of service, complicated in fact due to even more formidable language barriers. Again, the method of service must be permitted by the law of the country concerned. How that is to be ascertained is left unanswered.

i. Recorded delivery post, which is described here as "postal service",

ii. "Service via central authority". This means asking the Scottish Ministers to effect service. The office to contact is the Scottish Government Justice Directorate, Central Authority and Justice Law Team, St Andrew's House, Regent Road, Edinburgh.

iii. "Consular service". This requires that the applicant requests the U.K. Foreign and Commonwealth Office, Treaty and Nationality Department, Palace Street, London, to serve. As in 19.4 "This method can always be used" if the recipient is a British national.

iv. "Service by competent person". This means giving the papers to someone entitled to serve documents in that territory. This seems to be the same as "Direct service" under 19.4. It is unclear why the same descriptive term cannot be used throughout these Rules.

The rules in 19.4 about translations apply *mutatis mutandis* under 19.5 and indeed in 19.6 and 19.7.

19.6 A country with which the UK has a convention on the service of documents. The examples given in the rules are Libya, Algeria and the United Arab Emirates.

The rules prescribe simply that service must be carried out in the terms prescribed by the particular convention. Where it requires that a copy of the document be served in a language that the recipient will understand a Translation Certificate must be provided by the interpreter to say that the foreign language version is a correct translation of the English one. In all these three examples the language is Arabic, of course.

19.7 A country which does not fall into any of these categories.

The rules prescribe two possible methods of service, complicated due to language barriers;

Recorded delivery post. This must often be a truly token exercise, not much more reliable than service by notice on the S.C.T.S website. It does reflect the sad reality, however, that there is probably little point in bringing a simple procedure action against a sheep farmer in Tajikistan.

Using the means of service prescribed by the domestic law of that country. This is referred to as "personal service."

As has been noted, the envelope used to send the papers must bear a label stating that the envelope contains a document from the particular sheriff court in Scotland and that delivery cannot be made it is to be returned immediately to the sheriff clerk, whose address must be provided. If the country where service is to be made is not English speaking, such as Mali, the label must be in the local language, of which that country has over a dozen. This is so that the Malian post person will return the envelope promptly.

In reality, much of Part 19 prescribes procedure which is a hollow exercise, not much better than where the respondent's whereabouts are unknown. There are of course 13.5 and 13.6, which apply where a decree is granted in absence. These rules allow the respondent to apply to the sheriff to recall the decision. More likely, he will ignore the whole process.

CHAPTER ELEVEN

HOW TO MAKE A CLAIM

Part 3 comprises 3.1 to 3.13. It consists of eleven questions, namely 3.1 to 3.3 and 3.6 to 3.13 (3.4 and 3.5 having been revoked by amendment) to which there are then answers some of which can be regarded as directions and others as statements of guidance and information. This Part refers at some answers to other Rules within Part 3. So 3.2(1)(a) refers to 3.3, for example. Part 3 also refers to provisions of Parts 4, 6, 9 and 20. Part 3 of the rules was amended by Act of Sederunt on three occasions, in 2018 and by two Acts of Sederunt in 2022.

The key elements of Part 3 are 3.3 and 3.7 namely, and respectively, how is the Claim Form 3A completed and what is then done with it.

The Claim Form 3A will be most applicants' first point of contact with the procedure. The English equivalent is also named Claim Form. This document is also the foundation for the entire action, so it needs to be correct. It states that "The Simple Procedure Rules should be read alongside this form." As already discussed, there is a lot more to simple procedure than the Rules. The party litigant will find that out as soon as he tries to decide the rate of interest to be inserted in box A1 and discovers that the appropriate rate is not mentioned in the Rules. The norm is 8% *per annum* but this "judicial rate" is not always appropriate. There may be a contractual rate or the Late Payment of Commercial Debts (Interest) Act 1998 and its subordinate legislation may apply. Mercifully, however, the Scottish system is far more straightforward than that operating in Ontario, where the rate depends on the quarter of the year in which the action was raised. Also, there and in New South Wales, the tables differentiate between pre-judgment and post-judgment periods.

As long ago as May 2018 the Law Society of Scotland suggested in its Response to a consultation exercise that as regards the Claim Form "It may be helpful to clarify the rate of interest that is permissible." That has not happened.

Completing the Form 3A

The Form was altered quite significantly for actions brought after 31st May 2023, and for the better. Before that, the Form had three boxes, E.1, (witness list) E.2 (documents "including photographs" and E.3 (any other piece of evidence"). In effect this required the claimant to lodge a witness list including "what their relationship to the claim is" and an inventory of productions. There was clearly a desire to avoid the sheriff clerk's office becoming a store for tangible items such as rent garments; E.3 gave the example of damage to clothing and that "You do not need to bring a piece of evidence if the important point can be shown in some other way, e.g. by photographs."

The Law Society's 2018 Response regarded completion of the Claim Form at that time as being "time consuming and laborious, and the number of fields to be completed seems excessive." Now, the claimant is required "briefly [to] describe the essential facts about the story behind your claim". The word "story" is a little unfortunate, suggesting creativity. The claimant is directed by the terms of box E1 to provide key dates, a breakdown of money, he basics of any agreement, when he became aware of the claim, whether any payments were made or services provided and the like. This is all sensible and more in line with the requirements under Small Claim Rule 4.2, headed "Statement of Claim". This emphasised the need "to give the defender fair notice" with details of the basis of the claim including relevant dates and a description of goods and services.

Sheriff clerks differ in how much they expect of a Form 3A. In 2024 the author submitted such a Form to a sheriff court on the north side of a river only to receive an email rejecting it on the basis that "It is not clear how the sum sued for has been reached." In the author's view it was patently obvious and, in any event, it seemed that the clerk had gone beyond his remit under 3.1 (see below). The case concerned a consumer contract, so there was jurisdiction in the court of the domicile of both parties. In this case these were different courts. Indeed, they were in different sheriffdoms. The author amended the jurisdiction section of the Form, and no other part of it, to found on the domicile of the respondent rather than the claimant and sent the Form to the corresponding court on the south side of the river. It was accepted without any problem. Obviously, it was clear to the sheriff clerk there how the sum sued for had been reached. Or perhaps that clerk took the view that it was not her job to assess the form for relevancy as opposed to competency.

This lack of consistency is unfortunate but an inevitable feature of any system dependant on the human judgment of individual office holders.

Completion of the Form 3A highlights that, as discussed, simple procedure is front loaded, meaning that the claimant has to do a great deal of preparation and work at the early stage of the action as opposed to its later stages.

3.4 once asked What if there is more than one claimant and 3.5 enquired What if there is more than one respondent. The answer was that the claimant had to complete more forms, namely a Further Claimant Form and a Further Respondent Form. In the list of Forms these were given the names Form 3B and Form 3C respectively. Now Form 3A directs the claimant to complete its relevant page "multiple times".

Having a multiplicity of forms was pointless. It does not feature in summary cause procedure and it was absent from small claims too. There, if there are two pursuers their names and addresses are inserted into the appropriate box on the Claim Form. A similar method is adopted where there is more than one defender. It is really quite straightforward.

Where someone uses a trading name 3.6 allows that respondent to be sued under that name. 15.3(1) provides that a decision (decree) bearing that trading name may be enforced against that person by that name. There would be little point in obtaining such a decision otherwise.

Mention has already been made of the hazards of suing an unincorporated association. Equally, there are perils in raising an action against a person (to use that term loosely) using a trading name. The prospect should raise red flags and sound alarm bells for the same reason; such entities may change name at the drop of a hat. Reputable people generally do not unless they marry.

6.10 applies where the respondent uses a trading name. It is something of an oddity.

6.10(1) requires that if such a respondent has a place of trading within the sheriffdom service must be made there.

6.10(2) stipulates that if the respondent does not have a place of trading within the sheriffdom but has one somewhere else service may be made at the latter.

So if there is a simple procedure case in Glasgow and the respondent, Holofernes Homebrewing Supplies, has a shop in Sauchiehall Street and a warehouse in Motherwell there has to be service at the shop, whereas if the case is in Hamilton Sheriff Court there would have to be service at the warehouse. If the action is raised in Dunfermline the claimant has a choice. One has to ask where the rationale lies for this requirement.

Suing the wrong person

This is far more problematic than used to be the case. When small claims procedure was introduced in 1988 there was no internet, social media or email. Some might characterise this as being a Dark Age where inkwells, quills and parchment prevailed, largely unchanged since the days of Viscount Stair in the late 1600s. In fact, there was far more certainly about legal relationships and rights because paper was the only medium available. Businesses used headed notepaper. This showed detail such as the identity of company directors, a V.A.T. number, company registration number, registered address and the like. Also, it would bear a signature, a wet signature. People expected other paper records of a transaction, such as a receipt or a delivery note. The law itself encouraged the use of written evidence; until the Requirements of Writing (Scotland) Act 1995 it was incompetent to prove gift or loan other than by writing evidence (or "writ" as it was known).

Now, so many contracts are made using texts or smartphone messages where the only information as to identity of the other party is that he is a plumber named Billy with an eleven-digit phone number.

In suing a limited company it always pays to check and quote its registration number. The Simple Procedure Forms are to be commended for encouraging this practice; box C4 of the Claim Form 3A advises the reader to check the Companies House website for the full name and company registration number in order to describe the respondent, and box E3 in the Provisional Orders Application Form 20A does the same to describe the arrestee (here called a "third party") A limited company may change its name but its registration number identifies it as the same entity, just as Archibald Leach and Cary Grant were the same person.

Suing the right person is a crucial but often overlooked aspect of any litigation. Commonwealth small claims websites emphasise this, reflecting the fact, perhaps, that party litigants may struggle with the issue or not consider it adequately. The Ontario site stresses the importance of getting it correct, giving the example of where the plaintiff sues "Zoro Casey Roofing", obtains a decree and then on attempting diligence finds that the name is actually "ZC Roofing Ltd." As the site succinctly puts it "You have a judgment against the wrong party". It gives examples of unincorporated businesses; sole proprietorship or partnership and advises that one sues the business name, and the owner and partner as additional parties. The equivalent site in New South Wales warns that "You will waste time and money if you make the claim against the wrong person or business." This is very true.

Suing the correct person is crucial from the outset. It is possible to have a mistake corrected once the case has been raised. The court can be asked to take the wrong respondent out and have the correct one brought in instead. However, the court might refuse, dismissing the case, finding the client liable for the expenses and making her start all over again.

3.8 concerns interim orders relating to diligence. This is the first point in the rules at which primary legislation is mentioned. The statutory provisions in question are section 15A(1) of the Debtors (Scotland) Act 1987 in relation to arrestment on the dependence and interim inhibition and section 9A(1) of the Debt Arrangement and Attachment (Scotland) Act 2002 in relation to interim attachment. 3.8 refers the reader to Part 20 in relation thereto.

3.9 What will the court do with the Claim Form? requires the sheriff clerk (not the sheriff) to check the form to ensure that it does not possess "problems... [which] ... might include" being accompanied by the wrong fee, or being in the wrong court or seeking an incompetent remedy, such as a claim for more than £5000 or where the Claim Form is incomplete. Assuming that none of these problems exists the clerk is directed by 3.10 to issue a Timetable. This is very sparse, consisting of two dates, one for service and one for a response. Under summary cause procedure the sheriff clerk simply inserts Return and Calling dates into the Summons. There is no separate document entitled "Timetable".

3.11 provides that the period of notice must normally be 3 weeks between service of the Form 3A and the last date for a response. If, however, the respondent (the equivalent in England is known, incidentally, as a "defendant") does not live in a E.U. State the period must normally be 6 weeks. This reference to the E.U. is bizarre. The difference in period of notice is attributable to geographical distance, not political alliances. O.C.R. 3.6 and Summary Cause Rule 4.5 differentiate between Europe (21 days) and elsewhere (42 days). So should 3.11. Procedural rules should align across the levels of litigation to avoid creating discrepancies and anomalies over countries such as Switzerland or Turkey.

3.13 allows the sheriff clerk or a party to request to have the Timetable changed if there is a problem with service. Essentially this will be the equivalent of minuting for re-service.

CHAPTER TWELVE

INTERIM DILIGENCE

Part 20 consists of 20.1 to 20.9. This concerns diligence *ad interim*. Diligence in execution is the subject of Part 15.

Practitioners need to be aware of a couple of dangers; the client will be angry if an opponent alienates assets while a case is pending thereby making himself too impecunious to satisfy a decree. To avoid the wrathful client blaming his lawyer the latter must advise on the availability of interim diligence and its costs. Sheriff officers will charge around £100 to serve a bank arrestment, for example. The latest measure governing these costs is the Fees of Messengers at Arms and Sheriff Officers (Amendment) 2024. Secondly, from a self-preservation perspective it is better to ask and have the order refused than not to ask at all; the finger of blame can then be diverted towards the sheriff.

20.1 states that this Part is about provisional orders which protect or secure the claimant's position before the sheriff makes a final decision in a case.

Back in 1988, when small claims procedure was introduced, there was a wonderful form of protective diligence that a pursuer had in his armoury. This was a warrant to arrest on the dependence, there for the asking. It was hugely effective. A small claim pursuer and indeed the pursuer in summary causes and ordinary actions would crave and would be given automatically by the sheriff clerk such a warrant, regardless of the strength or merits of the case, the financial standing of the defender or the risk of his getting rid of assets or otherwise rendering a decree worthless.

Automatic warrant to arrest on the dependence was held in *Karl Construction v Palisade Properties Plc* SLT 2002 312 to be incompatible with the Human Rights Act. It was replaced by a mechanism which was designed so that the granting of the warrant was made a judicial rather than an administrative act. Now, it needs to be reasonable and justified by the circumstances of the specific case, rather than just granted as a matter of course. A key defect of the new procedure is that it is expected that the respondent will be given notice of the motion for warrant unless in exceptional circumstances. This notice obviously gives him time to transfer bank funds to his spouse, to take out cash and hide it under the mattress and otherwise to diminish or extinguish the funds which would otherwise be arrestable. The claimant's solicitor should always try to advance a reason why this diligence should be granted without notice. If that is refused the client has far less cause for complaint than if dispensation of notice had not been requested at all.

Where an order is granted without notice the legislation requires that there be a follow up diet to review it. This gives the defender a chance to seek recall.

Part 20 is badly worded in a number of respects.

Firstly, it is baffling why the adjective "interim" was not chosen instead of "provisional". The former is widely used in ordinary cause procedure but also in statutes. No court user ever refers to "provisional interdict" or "provisional inhibition", for example.

Most lawyers hearing "provisional" would think of provisional damages, a concept created by Section 12 the Administration of Justice Act 1982 which is different in principle and purpose to interim damages.

Secondly, "provisional orders" are not defined in Part 20. This is a failing; there are only three such orders and they can be described in short compass. However, to find a definition one has to consider the terms of the Provisional Orders Application Form 20A. Part C1 of the form asks, in the manner redolent of a waiter taking an order from a menu "What type of provisional order would you like the court to make?" before listing them. There are three. None includes the word "provisional". They are arrestment on the dependence and interim inhibition under Section 15A(1) of the Debtors (Scotland) Act 1987 and interim attachment under Section 9A(1) of the Debt Arrangement and Attachment (Scotland) Act 2002

20.2 provides that a claimant may request provisional orders by sending Form 20A to the court This can be either at the outset of the action (in which case the Claim Form has to be sent too) or subsequently but prior to the granting of a decision (i.e. decree). Form 20A serves two purposes; it is the application to the court but is also used to give notice to the respondent if notice is required. Accordingly, if the claimant is requesting a diet a copy of Form 20A must be sent by the claimant to the respondent unless he wants the orders granted without any notice having been granted (which is generally desirable for the reasons already given).

20.3 and the (lengthy) Form 20A regulate procedure as to diets.

The claimant who does not want a diet is directed by C2 of the Form 20A to section 15E(2) of the 1987 Act if he is seeking arrestment or inhibition on the dependence or section 9D(2) of the 2002 Act in the event of his seeking interim attachment.

In either scenario D1 and D2 requires the claimant to make a choice; he can ask that if the sheriff is minded to refuse the application the sheriff should fix a diet rather than dismissing the application. Or, he can indicate that even in such an eventuality he does not want a diet. In this event the sheriff will just refuse the application.

Section 15E(2) of the 1987 Act is headed "Hearing on application" (and, obviously, "hearing" does not mean a proof). It contains the criteria for granting the warrant. Essentially, these form a three point test whereby (a) the claimant must have "a *prima facie* case on the merits", (b) there must be "a real and substantial risk" that enforcement of a decision would "be defeated or prejudiced" by the debtor's insolvency or the likelihood of his removing, disposing of, burdening, concealing or otherwise dealing with" his assets and (c) it must be reasonable in all the circumstances including having regard to the effect of the warrant on "any person having an interest". The same test applies in terms of section 9D(2) of the 2002 Act, which is headed "Grant of warrant without a hearing".

The claimant who at the outset and for whatever reason wants a diet is directed by C2 of the Form 20A to section 15F(3) of the 1987 Act or section 9E(3) of the 2002 Act respectively. Ticking the second of the boxes at D1 indicates his request for a hearing, and the sheriff will fix one.

Further on Form 20A one finds E and F. The former of these is headed "Arrestment on the Dependence; Information about Third Party". The so called third party is defined as "the person who holds goods or money that belongs to the respondent", in other words the proposed arrestee. Details of this person (the form has space for one) must be provided.

This begs the question of whether this form corrals the applicant into restricting the diligence against specific parties. It does seem so. Putting "The Bank of Bechuanaland" at E appears to preclude service of an arrestment on "The Royal Bank of Nyasaland". In ordinary procedure there are no such restrictions; the litigant granted a warrant to arrest on the dependence may serve it on anybody, justified on the ground that very often he will have no idea where the funds are. A scattergun approach is sometimes the only option, with most of the impact being wide of the mark; quite often an arrestment will be served on four or so high street banks. Simple procedure appears designed to prevent this, and it is not at all clear why.

F concerns "Interested Persons" and requires that information be provided similar to that at D.

If an order is granted without a diet the court must assign a Provisional Orders Application Review Hearing and order the Claimant to intimate it to the Respondent. This is yet another example of a bad choice of terminology in the Rules. As we will see, in Part 12 "hearing" means "proof". Accordingly, the term should be avoided in Part 20. It might lead some to understand that a hearing on interim diligence will hear testimony from witnesses. That simply does not happen.

20.4 provides that a clamant must use a form Provisional Orders Hearing Notice Form 20B to intimate a diet to the respondent or an interested party. This is a short form which tells the respondent whether that diet is a "provisional orders hearing" under section 15F of the 1987 Act or section 9E of the 2002 Act, or "provisional orders review hearing" under section 15K of the 1987 Act or section 9M of the 2002 Act. These sections are quoted in the Form 20B.

20.5 allows an application to be made that the court reconsider an order already granted. This is done by lodging a Provisional Orders Reconsideration Hearing Form 20C

An order may be sought either by the respondent or an interested party. This can be in relation to any of the three protective diligences listed in at C1 of the Provisional Orders Application Form 20A. Form 20C explains at C3 that in relation to arrestment or inhibition on the dependence the court's powers are at section 15K of the 1987 Act and that in respect of interim attachment the applicable provision is section M of the 2002 Act.

20.6 asks "How can you ask the court to consider other applications about Provisional Orders?"

These "other applications about Provisional Orders" are stated as being those orders mentioned in Part 1A of the 1987 Act or Part 1A of the 2002 Act. This is another instance of where the Simple Procedure Rules clarify that they are not self-contained; one is directed to look at the legislation narrated.

Part 1A of the 1987 Act is headed Diligence on the Dependence and covers recall, restriction and variation of orders and challenges to the validity of the warrant with provision for the court to attach conditions such as the consigning of money at court or the finding of caution.

Part 1A of the 2002 Act is headed Interim Attachment and contains matters comparable to those in Part 1A of the 1987 Act but also unlawful acts in relation to attached articles (in relation to which reference is made to Section 21 of the Act which lies outwith Part 1A) and articles belonging to or owned in common with third parties.

Part 20.6 provides that anyone (party or arrestee) seeking such an order must apply using the procedure in Part 9, that is by lodging and intimating an Additional Orders Application (Form 9A).

20.6. 3 states that where the court receives "such an Incidental (sic.) Orders Application" a hearing must be assigned.

20.7 poses the question How are provisional orders made effective? Remember, there are three types.

20.7(2) relates to arrestment on the dependence. From the viewpoint of a court user this one is the easiest to fathom; reference is made to 20.8 and there are two forms. The first of these, the Arrestment Notice Form 20D has to be served on the arrestee ("third party"). This form will be served by sheriff officer and therefore practitioners do not need to be too concerned about the mechanics of how it is implemented unless they are consulted by the arrestee who need not, of course, be a bank. It could be another debtor of the respondent.

Form 20D does not simply alert the arrestee to the court's order, it requires the arrestee to take certain steps including calculating the respondent's Protected Minimum Balance in terms of section 73F of the 1987 Act thereby enabling the sum arrested to be stated in the form. The sheriff officer signs the arrestment section at D "in Her (sic.) Majesty's Name". E is headed "Duties of the Third Party" and requires the arrestee to retain the funds arrested and, in terms of section 73G of the 1987 Act, to disclose the situation to the claimant within 3 weeks using a form in Schedule 8 to the Diligence (Scotland) Regulations 2009. A copy of the disclosure must also be made to the respondent and anyone who owns or claims to own attached goods or to whom the attached money is due or claimed to be due. The form warns that failure to comply may attract a financial penalty under section 73H of the Act or might be dealt with as a contempt of court.

Once this process has concluded the sheriff officer completes the second form named in 20.8. This is the Confirmation of Formal Service of Arrestment Notice 20E, a very simple document, and this is sent to the court. Service must be by sheriff officer subject to the exceptions under Sections 2 and 3 of the Execution of Diligence (Scotland) Act 1926. This allows a solicitor to serve where no sheriff officer or messenger at arms is available. Whether any solicitor would wish to take on this responsibility is another matter.

20.7(3) relates to inhibition on the dependence. One could be forgiven for failing to remember that this procedure is meant to be capable of being understood by lay litigants. There are no forms provided. At this point the Simple Procedure Rules wisely seem to recognise their limitations. Instead, there is a statement that the procedure is governed by section 148(3)(b) of the Bankruptcy and Diligence (Scotland) Act 2007 and the Diligence (Scotland) Regulations 2009.

20.7(4) relates to interim attachment. Again, the provision is not user friendly. It states merely that regard has to be had to Chapter 1A of the Rules for Applications to the Sheriff Court under the Debt Arrangement and Attachment (Scotland) Act 2002. It is not easy to locate that Chapter online.

20.9 stipulates how sheriff officers serve an order for interim inhibition where the alleged debtor's address is unknown.

CHAPTER THIRTEEN

HOW TO RESPOND TO A CLAIM

Part 4 consists of 4.1 to 4.5, and is probably the best drafted part of the Rules. It is divided into 4.1 to 4.5 and consists of five questions to which there are then nine answers. As in previous Parts, some answers can be regarded as rules whereas others are statements of guidance and information. The most practical are 4.2 and 4.4. Respectively, these are how one responds and what is to be included in the Response Form 4A. Part 4 includes a flow chart which assists a respondent in knowing how to react to a claim. This is an extremely useful device and one which ought to be more widely deployed in other forms of litigation. Whoever receives the Timetable is left with very little doubt as to how he needs to respond and by when. Part 4 is largely self-contained, other than that the Time to Pay Application is derived from Part 5.

Times have moved on substantially from the days of the pre-2002 Summary Cause Rules when a defender merely had to advise that she was defending the case and could appear at the first calling without having given any notice whatsoever of her defence.

4.2 (1) states that the respondent must respond to the claim by the last date for a response. The meaning of this is to be found in 3.10 which provides for a Timetable, Form 3D. This is easy to follow, containing two dates, the latter of which is the last date for a response.

If the respondent does not lodge a Response Form or Time to Pay Application the applicant is entitled to ask for a decision (essentially a decree in absence) under 7.4(2). The respondent is then entitled to seek a recall of that decision under 13.7. This occurred in *Bell v Farmer and Farmer* [2023] SAC (Civ) 6 where the Sheriff Appeal Court had to decide whether there was a right of appeal against a refusal to recall a decision. The defender had failed to lodge a Response Form and decree was granted. An application was made to recall the decision but the sheriff refused it, also ruling that an appeal against that refusal would be incompetent. Sheriff Principal Anwar held that a decision to refuse to recall a decision was included in the definition of a "final judgment in a simple procedure case" (s82(1) of the 2014 Act) and was appealable. She also observed that once an appeal is marked the sheriff is *functus* and is not in a position to "entertain questions about the competency of the appeal." That is a matter for the appeal court.

4.2 (2) provides for the completion of a Response Form and 4.2(3) for a Time to Pay Application.

4.3 envisages three options; the respondent may either admit the claim and settle before the last date for a response, or admit the claim and ask for time to pay or dispute all or some of the claim.

4.3 (3) comprises the flow chart already mentioned. This innovation should be copied by other forms of procedure.

4.4(1) explains how the Response Form should be completed; it should contain the facts that are agreed, those where there is disagreement, why the claimant should not get that which he wants and what the respondent has done (if anything) to try to settle the matter. 4.4(2) requires the respondent to say if there ought to be any additional respondents. There is little encouragement towards prolixity here, although box D1, with reference to dates, agreement terms and so on, is comparable to the same box in the Claim Form 3A.

As with the Claim Form 3A, for post 31st May 2023 claims there is no requirement to lodge a witness list, inventory of productions or of real evidence.

4.5 requires the sheriff clerk to give the sheriff the Claim Form 3A, Response Form 4A and Confirmation of Formal Service

Unlike the position in England (where the form of response, N9B, is headed "Defence and Counterclaim") there is no provision to counterclaim under simple procedure. This is a surprising omission and an unfortunate one, because it deprives the defender of an easy mechanism to vindicate his rights and it flies in the face of trying to avoid a multiplicity of actions.

Under the original Small Claims rules, from 1988, it was not competent to counterclaim. The defender had to move to remit the action to the summary cause roll, where such procedure was and still is permitted under Chapter 10. The Small Claims Rules 2002 sensibly contained chapter 11 which allowed the defender to counterclaim. The draft Simple Procedure Rules did too, but this provision was dropped before the final rules were approved. This was because "cases so complex that a counterclaim procedure is required are likely to be remitted to Ordinary Cause procedure" (Scottish Civil Justice Council Report, June 2016). This reasoning is unconvincing. Apart from a few complications such as valuing the action (is it the aggregate of the sums claimed and counterclaimed?) it makes sense to hear all the evidence at one time, whether that is in a conjoined action or proof.

As matters stand, if the defender's position is that he is due a sum by the pursuer he has to plead "set off" and prove that the sum is indeed due. If he succeeds the most that he will achieve is having to pay nothing to the pursuer. However, he will not be able to use that decision actively to seek payment. He would have to raise a separate payment action and do so in time to try to obtain a conjoined proof. Otherwise, there would be duplication of costs and possibly the bringing into play of the doctrine of *res judicata.* None of this is conducive to simplicity or a good use of resources.

The absence of any provision to allow a counterclaim in simple procedure means that the respondent would have to raise a cross action. Can the two be conjoined? There is a difference between conjoining two actions and conjoining proofs. See *Macphail* Conjunction of Processes 13.46 to 13.48. The latter is recommended by Joint Minute and, failing that, the court can be asked to conjoin the processes themselves. In the context of simple procedure the former seems more complicated than simply having two hearings conjoined.

1.8(7) allows the sheriff to "combine separate cases, so that any discussion in court, case management discussion or hearing in the cases is held at the same time." Essentially, this power to conjoin allows procedural diets and proofs in separate actions to be held simultaneously.

The guddle that was *Slessor-Burnett v Stuart* 1990 SLT (Sh Ct) 62 arose from the fact that the original small claim rules did not allow counterclaim. The defender wanted to do so. The sheriff, no doubt trying to be pragmatic in the face of rules that restricted his options, granted decree and suspended extract to let the counter-action progress. On appeal the Sheriff Principal held that the principal claim should have been met with a set-off defence.

Part 5, comprising 5.1 to 5.7 applies where a claim is undisputed but where the respondent seeks to satisfy the sum sued for. An equivalent exists under English procedure too. An individual (not a limited company) respondent may apply for time to pay. Part 5 has been amended three times. However, there remain three key areas where there is a deficiency, and a solicitor must give advice;

a. Nowhere is it stated that time to pay directions are established by the Debtors (Scotland) Act 1987. This is in contrast to 3.8 which, we have seen, refers to primary legislation.

b. There is no warning that where a decree (or "decision" to use the simple procedure nomenclature) is granted subject to a time to pay direction it is still a decree in the same way as an unqualified (or "open" decree) and that it can affect the respondent's credit rating. An instalment decree is still a decree albeit one that is subject to qualifications. Never assume that clients know this. They need to be made aware that to avoid a decree passing they need to settle the claim extra-judicially, asking that it be paused (i.e. sisted) to implement the terms.

c. There is no guidance to either the claimant or the respondent as to what would be a reasonable offer. In the author's experience, most sheriffs in Glasgow would regard it as unreasonable if a pursuer had to wait more than two years to have his debt cleared, but some sheriffs have taken the view that one year was a good rule of thumb. The matter is entirely discretionary.

The rest of Part 5 deals with where an application is consented to or opposed. 5.5 appears to give the court discretion even if there is consent; it "may" be granted. If there is opposition a "time to pay hearing" (which is a diet, not a hearing) is assigned. If the claimant fails to consent or object the sheriff will decide the application by granting or refusing it; 5.7.

CHAPTER FOURTEEN

UNDISPUTED AND DISPUTED CASES, FIRST WRITTEN ORDERS AND CASE MANAGEMENT DISCUSSIONS

Part 7 comprises 7.1 to 7.8. being eight questions and twenty-eight answers. There are references to Part 12, 1.8 (11), (11A), (12) and (13) and Parts 5 and 12. Part 7 was amended in 2016, 2018 and 2022.

7.2 to 7.4 concern undefended actions (which means either that there is no Response Form or that there is only a Time to Pay Application). 7.5 to 7.8 govern defended actions, i.e where there is a Response Form.

Essentially there are four possibilities. These are governed by 7.2 to 7.5.

Form 4A (the Response Form) warns the respondent that if he does nothing "the court will almost certainly, if appropriate, award the claim to the claimant".

Section C of Form 4A then tells the respondent -in the following order – that she has three options;

Accept that the debt is due, accept that she must settle with the applicant, send the Form 4A to the court and applicant and then pay up by the time of the last date for a Response.

Dispute the claim (including challenging jurisdiction), send the Form 4A to the court and applicant by the last date for a Response and await orders from the sheriff.

Accept that the debt is due but send a Time to Pay Application to the court; a direction is made to "See Part 5 of the Simple Procedure Rules".

Whether the respondent does nothing or applies for a time to pay direction the case is undefended. When simple procedure was introduced nobody was clear as to the extent to which the sheriff had a locus to enquiry into the merits of an undefended claim. The matter was not clarified until the Sheriff Appeal Court heard three appeals in tandem, *Cabot Financial UK Ltd v Robert McGregor and against Liam Gardner and Kirsty Brown* [2018] SAC (Civ) 12 All three cases originated in Hamiliton sheriff court.

McGregor lodged a time to pay application and the claimant consented to it. The two other respondents did nothing and the claimant in essence sought open decree in absence.

Instead of granting an instalment decree and two open decrees the sheriff made an unless order (more of which later) requiring the claimant to lodge documents within 28 days. The claimant refused to do so, the cases were dismissed and the claimant appealed. None of the respondents entered process, leaving the Sheriff Appeal Court to appoint an *amicus curiae.*

The concept of *amicus curiae* ("friend of the court") is yet another component of the law of simple procedure that is absent from the Regulations, Rules and legislation. It is essentially the common law notion that it can be contrary to the interests of justice if a position is argued in court in the absence of a contradictor. An *amicus curiae* is not technically an agent of or counsel for the absent party nominally opposing the position advanced. In practice that person may well have absolutely no interest in the outcome of the matter; otherwise he would have entered appearance The *amicus curiae* is there not so much to play devil's advocate as to present a "neutral appraisal of the issues" or raise matters which might not come to the court's attention.

Pars judicis is that which a judge has a duty to do. This encompasses noticing whether the citation of a defender has been irregular. (*Hamilton v Murray and Co* (1830) 9 S 143.) It includes noting whether the court has jurisdiction to determine the case. This is so whether the action is defended or not and whether the defender raises the point or not. The Ordinary Cause Rules specifically provide at Rule 7(2)(2) that in an undefended action the sheriff must not grant decree unless it appears *ex facie* of the writ that jurisdiction exists. Although there is no equivalent in the simple procedure rules the sheriff's inherent jurisdiction at common law in undefended cases is unaltered by those rules. It is *pars judicis* to take a point of prescription because the right relied upon by the pursuer is non- existent and a decree founded upon it would be a legal nullity. It is not *pars judicis* to dismiss an action based on irrelevancy

The courts dislike incompetency. Summary Cause Rule 8(3)(1) allows the court to dismiss a case that is clearly incompetent. The general extent to which a court can note a matter of competency arose in the recent ordinary case of *McCandlish v Johnston and Sweeney* 2024 SAC (Civ) 17. The appeal court was required to hear a case alleging a breach of interdict, the terms of which were described by that court as "somewhat remarkable" and which "appeared to compel positive action" concerning the exercise of a servitude over land. The defenders were party litigants and "In the absence of argument we are not prepared to recognize this interdict as competent.".

7.2 applies where the parties settle before the last date for a Response Form. The claimant must do two things, within 2 weeks of the last date for a response;

i) send to the sheriff clerk an Application for a Decision Form. This is essentially a Minute for dismissal or decree. The sheriff may put the matter out by order for a diet at which there can be a discussion.

ii) send to the sheriff clerk evidence that the Claim Form was served.

A failure to do this will lead to dismissal under 7.2(4).

7.3 applies if there is a Time to Pay Application. It simply refers the reader to Part 5; "How to Ask for Time to Pay"

Under Small Claim Rule 8.2 the pursuer could intimate that he accepted the application in which case the case would not call. If he intimated that it was opposed it would call at the preliminary hearing. If he failed to react at all the sheriff was empowered to dismiss the action.

7.4 applies where there is no Response Form or Time to Pay Application.

Under Small Claim Rule 8.1 the pursuer had to minute for decree before the calling date otherwise the case would be dismissed. Similarly, under simple procedure the claimant "sends an Application for a Decision" (i.e minute for decree) within 2 weeks from the last date for a response or the sheriff must dismiss the case; 7.4(4) If the claimant makes an Application for a Decision in time the sheriff "may" make a decision awarding some or all claimed in the Claim Form or, if he considers that he cannot do so he may order the claimant to attend court "to discuss the terms of the decision."; 7.4(2) and (3) The limits on the court's interventionist approach in undefended cases was analysed by the Sheriff Appeal Court in the *Cabot Financial UK Ltd v McGregor, Garner and Brown* cases referred to above, heard as one appeal. Also relevant are *Santander Consumer (UK) Plc v Alan Creighton* and *Santander Consumer (UK) Plc v William Simpson* [2019] SAC (Civ) 36, two separate cases heard as one appeal, and *Clydesdale Financial Services Ltd v Wojcick* [2019] SC PER 29.

7.5 relates to Disputed Claims.

7.5(1) directs that the sheriff must consider the papers "in private" and 7.5(2) requires that the sheriff must send "first written orders" within 2 weeks of receiving the Response Form.

This requirement that there be an assessment in chambers differentiates simple procedure substantially from how the same exercise was conducted under small claims. It is worth considering how the latter were processed; under Small Claim Rule 9.1 the case had to call in open court at a diet named "the hearing". It was a procedural diet, not a proof.

In this respect the small claims system was very inefficient. At the hearing there might have been many dozens of cases put down to call at the one time, usually 10am. A multitude of solicitors loitered about whilst the sheriff read each summons one after another. One could be waiting all morning for a case to call. From a time management perspective it makes far more sense for this process to take place in chambers. In this regard simple procedure has been a huge improvement on that of small claims.

This issue was a matter of consultation when simple procedure was at its prototype draft stage. The proposal to have this exercise conducted privately was met with hostility by the Sheriffs' Association. It is interesting to note its Response in the Consultation that preceded the introduction of the Simple Procedure Rules (the final version of which differed from those at the Consultation stage). The Response stated that "We do not consider that a chambers consideration of the case and the written orders will result in the resolution of many cases prior to the [proof] hearing." and that "what is perhaps not fully appreciated by the drafter of the rules is the extent to which party litigants will fail to complete forms properly, will not understand the required factual or legal basis of their claim/defence or appreciate the evidence required to support this."

7.5(3) to (5) are to the effect that written orders need not be sent if the respondent submits that there ought to be "additional respondents". In that scenario the court may order service on such persons and then issue written orders once they have had time to lodge a response.

"first written orders" are defined in 7.6. There are five;

(a) Refer the parties to alternative dispute resolution. Oddly, and despite its being referred to on three separate occasions "Alternative dispute resolution" is not defined either in Regulation 3 or in the Glossary. However, it is doubtful if it covers remit to a person of skill. A definition is to be found in the Scottish Civil Justice Council's report "Access to Justice Literature Review. Alternative Dispute Resolution in Scotland

and other jurisdictions." from December 2014. This classifies A.D.R. under six headings, namely, negotiation, mediation (the most common), arbitration, conciliation (more interventionist than mediation) collaborative law (predominantly in divorce) and early neutral evaluation (ENE) which is a mixture of mediation and non-binding arbitration. *Churchill v Merthyr Tydfil County Borough Council* [2023] EWCA Civ 1416 provides an interesting analysis of the circumstances in which parties should be referred to mediation. The case concerned an outbreak of Japanese Knotweed. The defendant applied for a stay of the proceedings for mediation. Their Lordships considered the opinion of Lord Justice Dyson from a 2004 case that "to oblige truly unwilling parties to refer their disputes to mediation would be to impose an unacceptable obstruction on their right of access to justice." Also, they considered Article 6 and decided that it was not appropriate for the Court of Appeal to "lay down fixed principles" or "to provide a checklist or score sheet for judges to operate". Practitioners would find life easier if they did, of course.

(b) Fix a case management discussion. This is the equivalent of the old small claim hearing. Incidentally, the 1988 Small Claims Rules referred to it as a "preliminary hearing" and the proof diet was commonly referred to as the "full hearing". This was sensible. Unfortunately, and confusingly, the 2002 Rules referred to both these diets as the "hearing". The equivalent terms under the current Summary Cause Rules are "hearing" and "proof".

(c) Fix a hearing (i.e. a proof). This diet is governed by Part 12. Going straight to a hearing would happen if the issues had been laid out in the Forms 3A and 4A with sufficient lucidity as to render a case management discussion unnecessary. 1.8(10) empowers the sheriff to decide a case without a hearing.

(d) intimate that the sheriff is considering making a decision (i.e. granting decree) without a hearing and giving the parties an opportunity to change his mind.

(e) Dismissing the action or granting a decision using the sheriff's powers under 1.8. There are four specific powers that can be invoked, (11), (11A), (12) and (13). They all allow dismissal or decision in whole or in part where the sheriff considers that the claim or defence (or part thereof) have "no real prospect of success" or where there is incompetency. It would appear that the sheriff can dispose of an action under (e) without requiring to give the parties a chance to make representations. The term "real prospect of success" was considered in the judicial review case of *Ochiemhen v Secretary of State of the Home Department* [2016] CSOH 20

7.7 defines the Case Management Discussion and sets out that which can happen at one. In broad terms the answer is that just about anything can happen. Practitioners need to be careful and well prepared in case the action is decided there and then against one's client who then promptly goes to study the S.L.C.C.'s website.

The stated purposes of the diet is to discuss the Claim and the Response, clarify any concerns that the sheriff may have, assign a hearing (proof) and give the parties guidance and orders about witnesses and documents for the hearing. The sheriff may discuss A.D.R. with the parties and direct them to it. The second principle of 1.2, that the "approach of the court to a case is to be as informal as is appropriate" should not lead to lawyers letting down their guard.

Small Claim Rule 9.3 stated that the equivalent hearing there "shall be conducted as informally as the circumstances of the claim permit". In *Dunn v Hall 1990 S.C.L.R. 673* Sheriff Principal Nicholson observed that the rule "does not confer a wholly unfettered discretion on the sheriff and did not allow a decision to be taken "in an injudicious manner or upon the basis of material which is plainly inadequate to support any kind of decision." This would encompass deciding a case on the basis that "success would go to the party who first addressed him in court."

This prohibition on arbitrary decision making would extend also to proofs. The sheriff cannot decide a case by tossing a coin or making a random selection from a deck of cards, despite the 1.8 (3) power entitling the sheriff, with seeming omnipotence, to "do anything or give any order considered necessary to decide the case."

7.7(4) allows the sheriff to do anything that could be done at the proof hearing, which would include granting a decree. If there is no appearance by one or both parties one has to look at 12.5; a party's absence may result in dismissal or a decision (i.e. decree). Recall procedure is provided for by 13.5. Alternatively, the sheriff could continue the diet for an appearance. Sometimes there can be good reasons for non-appearance and these may not be apparent at the time; a sudden trauma or sickness, for example.

If there is no jurisdiction in a Summary Cause the sheriff can transfer it to the correct court under Rule 16.1. In an ordinary action (Rule 26.1) the sheriff can transfer but only on the motion of a party (the pursuer, one would assume), it cannot be done *ex proprio motu.*

7.8 defines the (proof) hearing, which it does in the most useless way imaginable;

"The purpose of a hearing is to help the sheriff to resolve the dispute between the parties".

Exactly the same definition could apply to the Case Management Discussion.

CHAPTER FIFTEEN

INTERLOCUTORS

Part 8 comprises 8.1 to 8.5 There are five questions and eleven answers. The relative form is Form 8A, entitled Order of the Sheriff. As with all the forms, it is to be found in Schedule 2.

This Part is a convoluted mess, a mixture of platitude and chaos which causes confusion where it need not exist. There was no equivalent in the Small Claims Rules and there is none in the Summary Cause Rules either.

On the face of it, Part 8 tries to be helpful. Orders appear to be synonymous with interlocutors. Perhaps it was felt that "interlocutor" had the potential to confuse; dictionaries advise that the word denotes a person rather than a statement, order or decree of a court. Whatever the reason, "interlocutor" is absent from the Simple Procedure Rules.

"Orders" are defined (after a fashion) at 8.2. "What are orders?" is met with the answer that "orders are the way that the sheriff uses the powers of the sheriff to manage or decide a case." This is obvious.

The method or manner of the giving of orders is stated in 8.2. This provides that the order can be in an "Order of the Sheriff Form" – which is Form 8A although that is not stated – or in person.

The Order of the Sheriff Form is contained in Schedule 2. That schedule is not mentioned anywhere in Part 8.

8.3 deals with "standard orders". This is where matters start to go awry. The sheriff can make

(a) a standard order

(b) an amended version of a standard order or

(c) an order customised to the case.

The structure here is odd; orders under (c) are clearly not standard orders (amended or otherwise) and one has to wonder why they are included under that heading. Indeed, one wonders why the rules include the concept of "standard orders" at all. An order assigning a case management hearing is a standard order but one referring the parties to A.D.R. is not. (see below). However, this distinction between standard and non-standard seems to have no practical purpose.

8.4 provides for "unless orders". These are defined as orders whereby "unless" someone does something the sheriff will make a decision including dismissal or making an award in favour of the claimant. They could equally be described as "Or Else" orders or peremptory orders. An unless order is an ultimatum. They are totally absent from ordinary and summary cause procedure and small claims procedure had no equivalent although the court has always been able to assign peremptory diets at which someone had to appear or be represented under pain of decree or dismissal if he did not.

Unsurprisingly, given their unprecedented and novel character, unless orders have not been without their problems. *Nathan Blair v Heather Baird* [2021] SAC (Civ) 13 found itself in the tabloids ("Scots neighbours in year-long court battle over 70 inch plasma TV"; *Daily Record* 28th March 2021). In it, the sheriff had made an unless order requiring the respondent to hand over a television set. When this did not happen a decision (i.e. decree) was granted. This was appealed and one of the issues that arose was how an unless order is supposed to be served on someone who is not present when it is granted – as happened in this case. The Sheriff Appeal Court ruled that it should be served by recorded delivery or sheriff officer service and if the party against whom it is directed is furth of Scotland the provisions of Part 19 should be used.

In *Ravensby Glass Co Ltd v Lifestyle Glass Design Ltd* [2019] SAC (Civ) 15 one of the points of appeal focussed on the sheriff's ordering the pursuer to provide information, that information not having been provided and there having been no sanction imposed in consequence of that failure. The appeal court observed that the order had not been an unless order and so there was no issue arising from the failure to comply with it. Further, any suggestion that an unless order should have been made was rejected, Sheriff Cubie (as he then was) stating that "Such an order should be used sparingly."

Strangely named terms are nothing new. Section 101 (now repealed) of the Sheriff Courts (Scotland) Act 1907 provided that where there was no interlocutor pronounced in a case for a year and a day "it shall be taken to have fallen asleep". It would then be "necessary to have the cause wakened before any further procedure" could take place (*Dobie on Sheriff Court Practice* 1952 p 242) The same phenomenon happened too in the Court of Session until 1965; *McLaren* has a whole chapter quaintly headed "Motion to Waken" with a paragraph on "A Sleeping Process".

Unless orders are another innovation of dubious value. Any distinctively peremptory nature possessed by unless orders is undermined by 8.5, which states that where the party does not follow an order the sheriff may dismiss or award something to the claimant. It is unclear whether the "order" referred to in 8.5 has to be one of the "unless orders" of 8.4. If not, 8.4 is otiose. If so, 8.5 is.

Paragraph 3(1) of the 2016 Regulations (not the Rules) is headed Interpretation of the Simple Procedure Rules. This provides, *inter alia* that "form" means one of those listed in Schedule 2 and that "standard order" means one of the standard orders in Schedule 3. That latter schedule, which refers to Regulation 3(1), comprises thirteen documents, SO1 to SO14 (there is no SO4).

Despite their appearance these documents cannot be called "forms" because they are contained in Schedule 3, not 2. They are narrations of standard orders and bear the heading "The Simple Procedure Order of the Sheriff" with the specific type below in much smaller print. They are essentially the contents to be inserted into Form 8A, which is listed in Schedule 2. Form 8A is little more than an empty vessel into which the court may pour one of the standard orders.

It is astonishing that this needlessly elaborate treatment of orders was ever considered an appropriate method of constructing interlocutors. One assumes that this use of templates is intended to facilitate the use of online processes. Yet, one yearns for the genuine simplicity of the Small Claims Rules.

Also provided in the list below (but not in the standard order documents themselves nor in Part 8) are the Rules to which these thirteen Form 8A contents relate.

SO1; Response Form received: ordering a case management discussion – 7.6(1)(c)

SO2; Response Form received: ordering a hearing – 7.6(1)(c)

SO3; Response Form received: Decision without a hearing – 7.6(1)(d)

Note that 7.5 and 7.6 refer to "first written orders". Accordingly, the three orders above are both standard orders and first written orders. However, there are two other first written orders possible under 7.6, namely (1)(b), referring the parties to A.D.R. and (1)(e), dismissing a case or deciding a claim under Rules 1.8(11), (11A), (12) or (13) where there is "obviously ... no real prospect of success" or where the claim or response "will not succeed because it is incompetent" . These two are therefore not standard orders, and there is nothing about them in Schedule 3.

There is no "SO4".

SO5; Transferring a case between courts – 17.2

SO6; Unless order – 8.4

SO7; Application to Pause

SO8; Application to Restart

SO9; Paused case – unless order – 9.7(2)

SO10; Order to recover documents – 10.6(1)

SO11; Special order to recover documents – 10.9(1)

SO12; Ordering an expenses hearing – 14.4(2) to (5)

SO13; Application to Recall received: ordering a discussion in court – 13.6(4)

SO14; Case with additional respondent under 7.5(4): procedure and timetable

CHAPTER SIXTEEN

MOTIONS

Part 9 is headed **Applications** and consists of 9.1 to 9.9

This entire part was created in May 2023 by Act of Sederunt 2022. There are nine questions and twenty-two answers. This is regarding applications that parties can make to do things in addition to those in Part 8. This is essentially a Part regarding Motions.

The rules refer to "Pausing and restarting cases" In the parlance of the Court of Session, ordinary, summary and small claims procedure this means sisting cases and recalling sists. Why that terminology was not retained in the interests of consistency is baffling. Reference has already been made to strange terms. At the consultation stage, when the draft Simple Procedure Rules were released, the proposal was to "freeze" and to "unfreeze" a case. The latter could as well as been to "thaw" a case. In any event, this language from the prototype rules was not ultimately adopted.

Sisting can mean "convening", as a representative or a mandatory or it can mean staying or suspending proceedings. As regards the latter this traditionally meant that an action would remain suspended unless and until a party had the sist recalled. If that did not happen the case could remain sisted indefinitely. In ordinary cause personal injury cases O.C.R. 36.H1(3) requires that a sist must be for a definitive period. At the time this provision was introduced many thought that this so-called sist was actually a continuation. Simple procedure has not followed this practice of stipulating a time limit when the case is sisted/paused. Instead, however, the situation must be reviewed after 6 months (see below).

Simple procedure originally asked;

9.2 How can a party ask for the progress of a case to be paused?, and

9.4 How can a party ask for a paused case to be restarted?

And directed that distinct Forms, 9A and 9B be used. This was all repealed for cases commencing after 31 May 2023. Now, there is a new multi-purpose Form 9A "Additional Orders Application" which enables a party to apply for either a pause or a restart. This is achieved by the form containing options which the party ticks. There are also tick boxes to enable the form to be used to apply to amend the Claim Form or the Response Form or to recover documents.

The use of this multipurpose document, Form 9A is a sensible amendment to the rules. The court will deal with an application to pause and an application to restart by issuing a Form 8A (Order of the Sheriff) combined with an order in terms of SO7; Application to Pause or SO8; Application to Restart.

9.7 of the amended rules asks What can the court do with a paused case? The answer is that once a case has been paused for six months the sheriff clerk is to draw this to the attention of the sheriff. The court will then issue a Form 8A including an unless order, all in terms of SO9.

9.8 Additional respondent

Natural misfortunes befall us all. The most extreme of these would be death itself. Writing in 1952, *Dobie* refers to the notion of civil death; "A person under sentence of death and who is thus civilly dead, can neither be a pursuer nor a defender. Neither can a person who has been outlawed". Artificial entities can of course perish far less dramatically, through administrative steps or inaction.

Where a party dies or loses capacity or becomes bankrupt during the dependence of an action it necessarily falls to someone else to choose to take on the mantle to enable the case to continue. Either the other party can move to sist a representative of the deceased or incapax or the representative can apply to be sisted as a new party or, in a bankruptcy, the trustee can take over the conduct of the action. In any event, the procedure can be complicated in relation to liability for expenses, the capacity in which the new party is acting and so on.

The Small Claims Rules 2002 had a chapter, number 14 headed "applications for sist of party and transference" which explained the position quite simply "where a party dies or becomes legally incapacitated". 14.1(1) was to let a party sist himself whereas 14.1(2) was to transfer the cause against someone else. In other words, the former empowered the representative and the latter the remaining party, usually the pursuer. In that regard, however, it should be remembered that it was competent under small claims procedure to counterclaim whereas in simple procedure it is not.

There are only two relevant rules under simple procedure.

9.8 asks "How can a person become an additional respondent in a case?" and provides that the person may apply.

9.9 poses the question "What can happen if a party dies or becomes legally incapacitated?" and answers to the effect that a person who asserts a right to represent can apply by an Additional orders Application.

Both scenarios envisage a non-party seeking to become a party.

9.8 applies where someone chooses to join an existing applicant and 9.9 is where someone elects to step into the breach left by the death or incapacity of an existing applicant.

Neither of them deals with an existing party looking to bring someone in. Say, for example, the respondent dies and the applicant wishes to continue the case against the executor. This was covered by Small Claim Rule 14.1(2) but does not appear to be specifically accommodated in the Simple Procedure Rules at all. However, there is always 1.8 (3), enabling the sheriff to "do anything or give any order considered necessary to decide the case."

CHAPTER SEVENTEEN

EVIDENCE

Part 10 is headed **Documents and other evidence** and consists of 10.1 to 10.11

Firstly, at the time of writing the temporary justice measures introduced by the Coronavirus (Recovery and Reform) (Scotland) Act 2022 are likely to be extended to 30th November 2025. These include restrictions on the use of physical documents in litigation. These provisions need to be checked carefully to ensure compliance with them.

Part 10 deals with two entirely separate processes, namely lodging productions and recovering documents (in that order; chronology would dictate that it is the wrong order). Linked to recovery of documents it also covers the exercise known as specification of documents and the granting of commission and diligence.

Small Claims Rules 17 and 18 were headed "Productions" and "Recovery of Documents" respectively, reflecting the reality that these are not synonymous. Terms matter. A document is not a production unless it is lodged. Conventionally (but not in simple procedure) it does not become evidence unless it is probative or until it is spoken to by a witness.

It is worth discussing at this point the notion of evidence, given that the heading of Part 10 is both misleading and also illustrative of the problems of dealing with low value claims in a court rather than in a tribunal or other less formal forum.

The whole concept of evidence, as so understood, is one that is wholly confounded by the Simple Procedure Rules, to the extent that to use the term is practically meaningless. The law of evidence had been hugely eroded in the last forty years, firstly by the Civil Evidence (Scotland) Act

1988 which removed the need for corroboration and allowed hearsay, and by the Requirements of Writing (Scotland) Act 1995 which allowed oral proof of matters which had previously required writing, such as loans and gifts. Evidence which at one time would have been inadmissible is now admissible but given lesser weight. There is still a distinction between probative (now known as "self-proving") and non-probative documents but under simple procedure these features are of such greatly diminished importance that to speak of evidence at all is misconceived.

Documentary Evidence is a part and parcel of almost all litigations. Some complex rules of evidence apply in ordinary procedure where there are copy documents. *Japan Leasing (Europe) plc v Weir's Trustee (No 2)* 1998 SC 543 concerned the status of a copy of a contractual document. There was a discussion over the "best evidence rule" and whether the copy document was admissible as evidence of the contents of the original. The Inner House held that it was not, and that Section 2 of the 1988 Act (which provides that evidence is not to be excluded solely because it is hearsay) does not apply to a contractual document as opposed to a past statement by a person. The solution to the issue in that case lay in Section 6, which allows a copy to be admissible as long as it has been authenticated by the person who made the copy of the original document.

Consideration of these tricky provisions has been swept away in relation to simple procedure. Section 77 of the 2014 Act boldly states that "Any enactment or rule of law that prevents evidence being led on grounds of inadmissibility before a court of law does not apply in simple procedure cases."

According to conventional Scots law, a document might constitute evidence or it might not, depending upon its nature. For example, an extract from the Register of Birth, Marriages and Deaths which states that Jock Lewes died on 30th December 1941 is evidence of that fact because such a document is probative; it does not require a witness to speak to its being genuine. On the other hand, a photocopy of the extract is not probative. Neither is a tradesman's quotation, a receipt, a delivery note, an email, a text or a screensaver image of an entry on social media. These all need a witness to state on oath or affirmation (although see below) that he instructed, issued, received, observed or otherwise interacted with the document. Even then, the evidence might be light in weight. Nevertheless, there are clear rules of evidence, which lawyers are trained to understand. Every solicitor knows that a document is not, *per se*, evidence of anything unless it is probative. The heading of Part 10, namely "Documents and other evidence" would have been more accurate had it been prefixed by "Self-proving".

Alternatively, the Rules should avoid the term "evidence" at all and use a less precise term, such as "material".

About the only form of civil action left where any evidential formalities remain is divorce; this requires sworn evidence, usually in the form of affidavit, and there needs to be corroboration. In addition, extract marriage and, if applicable, birth certificates need to be docquetted and lodged; photocopies will not suffice, let alone scans attached to emails.

Under simple procedure, solicitors need to tread carefully as regards evidence, simply because the rules (such as there are any) are unpredictable and uncertain in any given case. It seems clear that "evidence" is used in the Rules in the colloquial or layperson's sense rather than in its technical sense according to Scots law. That is unhelpful.

Rules beyond Part 10 illustrate the hazards of trying to pin down the meaning of "evidence" in the contact of these Rules. By way of illustration;

12.6(1) states that "before evidence is heard, the sheriff must explain … the way the sheriff has decided to consider evidence at the hearing"

12.6(3); "The sheriff may decide whether the evidence of a witness is to be taken on oath or affirmation or not." Leaving aside the question of why it would ever be appropriate for a witness not to be expected to take the oath or to affirm this rule infers that an individual who speaks is thereby giving evidence.

These issues just discussed are not pedantic or merely academic; they have real practical consequences. One of the first steps that has to be undertaken in the preparation of any litigation is an assessment of the sufficiency of evidence.

For example, suppose a client has a claim for a breach of missives, and one of the heads of loss is the bill incurred by way of temporary accommodation costs at a bed and breakfast. If the client has nothing in writing the solicitor has to advise on the extent to which written material should be produced and, if the client does not possess it, the steps that should be undertaken to recover it. Taking steps costs money.

Either way, this part is arranged in two quite distinct elements, and not the correct way about. The first concerns "How can you lodge documents and other evidence with the court?" and the second is "How can a party recover documents to lodge them with the court?"

The latter is covered by 10.6 to 10.11. These are concerned with the process otherwise known as a specification of documents. It is appropriate to consider them before 10.2 to 10.5

Essentially, the procedure tries to mirror that in Ordinary Procedure but with language that it is assumed laypersons will understand. So, for example, the term "haver" is avoided. Unfortunately there are problems in translation and gaps in the explanation.

In addition, the concept of tangible "documents" is rapidly becoming redundant due to the increase in paperless systems. That may be why there is no equivalent under simple procedure to Summary Cause Rule 18.6 entitled "Warrants for production of original documents from public records". As commissioner, the author and an I.T specialist once carried out a "dawn raid" search of the office of a financial advisor in Glasgow. This included requesting access to filing cabinets with a warning that any obstruction would be reported to the sheriff. However, the cabinets were barren, and the office staff advised that all the data was stored remotely and electronically. This gave rise to a query over the extent to which the haver was required to hand over only that which he already had in tangible form or whether he was required to retrieve and encapsulate the electronic data and provide that. Ultimately, of course, it largely depends on the wording of the specification. Any commissioner acting cautiously will adhere strictly to the remit established by the sheriff's warrant, especially as acting *ultra vires* will leave him exposed to a claim of wrongful diligence, breaching confidentiality and the G.D.P.R. The same risks exist under simple procedure.

Under ordinary procedure a party may ask initially for the appointment of a commissioner rather than having to use Optional Procedure whereby the request to produce the documents is communicated directly to the haver with no commissioner involved. This is why the procedure is described as optional. By contrast, under simple procedure the party must try the direct method first and only if it fails can a commissioner be deployed. Given that specification of document procedure is generally used only where a haver is unwilling to co-operate this restriction seems unwise and likely to waste time.

To obtain a warrant to recover documents 10.6 requires the applicant to submit a Form 9A (the Additional Orders Application already discussed) which requires to state the documents that the party seeks to recover, the person who has them and the reason why recovery is sought. Accordingly, there is one application whereas under ordinary procedure there are two distinct documents, namely a motion and a separate list of items the latter of which is headed "Specification of Documents".

There are other curious contrasts between simple and ordinary procedure. Under the latter the party making the application names within the motion the name and address of the proposed commissioner but not the haver or havers. Under simple procedure the haver is named but not the commissioner.

If the Form 9A application is granted (which might be in chambers or at a diet assigned for consideration of the matter) 10.7 provides that the party must serve it on the person holding the documents. The latter must then lodge the documents with the sheriff clerk and, if confidentiality is claimed, they must be lodged in a sealed envelope marked confidential. 10.8 states that where the latter course is followed the party has to enrol another Form 9A for permission to open the envelope. This, of course, mirrors the same process followed in ordinary procedure. The decision as to whether the documents may be accessed is one for the sheriff. 10.8(6) states that the "sheriff may order parts ... to be redacted". The rules do not say who is to redact but in the absence of a commissioner it would presumably have to be the sheriff. One matter is clear; "It is not for the party or haver to determine unilaterally what can and cannot be produced"; Sheriff A Cubie (as he then was) in the social work referral case reported as 2020 SC GLA 40. In that case the haver was heavily criticised for undertaking redaction of documents which had been ordered to be produced under specification procedure.

10.9 applies where the haver does not respond to the service of the warrant. The party must lodge another Form 9A seeking a "special order to recover documents" 10.10 describes the appointment of a commissioner (described as such). 10.10(3) states with remarkable brevity that "The commissioner must carry out the recovery of documents mentioned in the order." In term of advising parties and the commissioner this is wholly inadequate. The position should be contrasted with Ordinary Cause Procedure; O.C.R. 28(4) is headed "Execution of commission and diligence for the recovery of documents" and sets out clearly the steps which require to be taken.

The Simple Procedure Rules give no indication of how a commissioner is paid or how he is to report to the sheriff. Summary Cause Chapter 18 is far more informative, including references to the administration of oaths to the shorthand writer and haver. There is also provision there for the taking of parole evidence to lie *in retentis*, a matter which is completely absent from the Simple Procedure Rules.

Solicitors need to warn clients of the potentially high costs of having a commissioner appointed. This is a risk which is often overlooked. Having been a commissioner many times the author knows how a commission can spiral in terms of time and cost. The commissioner will normally be solicitor, charging around £200 per hour plus VAT. If one knows that it will take an hour to hold a commission and another hour to collate the documents recovered and to file them into a report the expense of the exercise can be estimated reasonably easily. However, one often does not know what will be produced by the haver. One often knows neither the size of the haystack nor the number or location of the needles. The author once had to retrieve architectural drawings and plans and was handed a disk which contained thousands of files the vast majority of which fell outwith the parameters of the specification. One file opened to reveal an index of ten or more each of which split in turn into a multitude. The recovery process took at least ten hours, generating a bill of thousands of pounds. That was an ordinary action but the same arduous exercise could occur in a simple procedure case in the context of which such an expense is completely disproportionate. In addition, due to the constraints on recovering expenses, including such outlays, the client is at risk of being severely out of pocket.

10.11 concerns where confidentiality is claimed. The procedure resembles that prescribed by 10.8.

There is no equivalent under simple procedure of Summary Cause Rule 18.7, "Letters of Request" to a foreign court or tribunal to take evidence. To switch to a forum where it would be competent it would be an option to seek a transfer to ordinary procedure under 17.2. However, the costs of such an exercise need to be carefully considered.

10.2 to 10.6 govern how documents (in other words productions) are to be lodged. These must be read in conjunction with the Sheriff Principals' Guidance for Court Users, Electronic submission of documents, 14th October 2022 which requires, for example, that all documents should be submitted using Civil Online. Only in exceptional circumstances should documents be lodged initially in hard copy, but hard copies must be lodged prior to any hearing (i.e. proof).

10.2 requires that a List of Evidence Form (an Inventory of Productions) be lodged and intimated at least 2 weeks before the hearing (proof). At the same time the documents themselves must be lodged, and copies sent to the other parties. If a party turns up at the hearing with other documents the sheriff may refuse to consider these; 10.3. There is an interesting distinction made in 10.4 between solicitors and their assistants on one hand and those not legally represented on the other. The former may borrow documents but the latter may not; they are permitted to inspect them at the sheriff clerk's office and, where possible, to copy or photograph them. 10.5 requires the sheriff clerk to keep documents for four weeks or for as long as a case is under appeal. Thereafter, unless the documents are uplifted within a fortnight they may be destroyed.

Part 11 is headed **Witnesses** and comprises 11.1 to 11.8

For a set of rules that professes to be user friendly it is far cry from the genuine simplicity thatexisted under Small Claims. Part 11 illustrates how the court rules have ballooned over the years. In the Small Claims Rules 1988 one finds one rule, numbered 16 and headed "Witnesses". It consists of six lines of a mere ninety-five words. In the 2002 Rules this had expanded to three rules, 17.4 to 17.6 and totalling thirty-two lines. Under simple procedure this line count has almost doubled; Part 11 consists of an unwieldy sixty-three lines.

In some systems, such as in New South Wales, the norm is for witness statements to be lodged and for submissions to be made on those. By contrast, simple procedure in Scotland still follows the traditional method of calling individuals to give parole evidence and to be cross-examined.

11.2(1) requires that parties send the court and each other a List of Witnesses Form 11A at least two weeks before the hearing.

11.2 (3) states that a "party only needs to cite a witness to appear ... if the party is unable otherwise to arrange for that witness to appear." This is a meaningless statement. Often one will not know whether the witness appears until the day of the proof itself, by which time it is too late to cite. 11.2 (3) seems to be designed to discourage citations, but it is unclear why. Formal citation is often no more expensive than sending an informal letter. It shows that the party citing means business. It is seen as treating a matter seriously. Witnesses often want a citation. It proves to an employer that they need to take time off work to attend court. More importantly, it protects the solicitor. Assume that a lawyer is instructed to call a witness and he merely writes to or emails that person to advise that the client wishes him to attend at, say, Elgin sheriff court on 18th March 2025 at 10am. Let us assume further that the witness fails to turn up. 12.3(5) states that "the sheriff must not continue a hearing to another day solely because a witness did (sic.) not appear." So, the client can be compelled to run a proof in the absence of an essential witness- this almost happened to the author in Glasgow sheriff court about ten years ago, even though a formal citation had been sent. This is not an innovation of simple procedure, however; Small Claim Rule 1988 16(2) stated that the court should not discharge a proof solely because a witness fails to attend.

If the hearing proceeds without the witness and the client loses there is a good chance that he will blame this on the absence of the witness - whether or not he would probably have lost anyway – and then question will arise as to whether the lawyer did enough to ensure that the witness would show up. If no citation was sent a complaint may follow. If one wishes to find out whether an S.L.C.C case handler thinks that a citation should have been sent then by all means do not cite witnesses. Otherwise, it ought to be done.

Where citation is deployed 11.2 (4) requires that it be by means of "formally serving" a Witness Citation Notice Form 11B upon the witness. Formal service is of course a term of art, one whose meaning is stipulated by Rule 18.

As regards the timing of citation 11.2 (5) states that formal service must be least three weeks before the hearing. Given that a List of Witnesses Form 11A need only be lodged two weeks before, a witness could validly be cited 18 days before the hearing and there might not yet be any such form produced.

11.3(2) states that if a witness who is cited fails to appear the sheriff may order the witness to be brought to court. The brevity of this rule belies its practical complexity. In ordinary procedure this step is known as issuing letters of second diligence. It is rarely used, for good reason. The author once conducted a summary cause proof in which a witness who was cited failed to appear and in which the sheriff issued such letters *ex proprio motu.* The case was an anti-social behaviour eviction action brought by a housing association in the south west of Glasgow. The witness was a housing officer who could – if he had wanted to – have given evidence of the tenants' dealing in drugs. He refused to attend and advised that if compelled to do so by sheriff officers he would state in evidence that he knew nothing. His reasoning was simple; he would rather perjure himself than have his legs broken. The point is this; if a party has to go to the lengths of having a witness brought to court by officers that witness is likely to be so reluctant or fearful that his evidence is likely to be unpredictable at best, hostile at worst.

Extraneous to the Rules, Regulation 4(1)(d) applies in situations where the sheriff orders that a witness be brought to court; it allows an award of expenses to be made against such a witness. O.C.R 29.9(2) is the equivalent measure under ordinary procedure.

11.4 asks "How will the court treat a child witness?" and provides for a Child Witness Notice, Form 11C. "Child" is not defined in the Glossary, but section 11 of the Vulnerable Witnesses (Scotland) Act 2004 defines a child as anyone under 18. The definition was originally a person under 16 but the 2004 Act was amended and the age was raised two years by section 22 of the Victims and Witnesses (Scotland) Act 2014. The Form 11C is designed to draw to the attention of the court that there is a child witness. The sheriff will then either require that special measures be put in place or not. This decision can be made with or without a hearing. The Form 11C requires the person completing it to express a view about whether special measures should be deployed and, if so, which one, but ultimately the matter is one for the sheriff's judgment as to what is most appropriate. The Form 11C has spaces for the insertion of the child's own views and those of her parents.

11.5 relates to other vulnerable witnesses and creates the Vulnerable Witness Application, Form 11D. Essentially, the sheriff has to decide whether to direct that special measures be put in place and, if so, those to be used. Its terms mirror those of the Form 11C.

The terms of 11.6, 11.7 and 11.8 all apply to both child and other vulnerable witnesses for the purposes of 11.4 and 11.5

11.6 defines "special measures" for the purposes of 11.4 and 11.5. There are four; allowing the evidence to be given to an "independent person" (i.e. a commissioner), by live tv link, from behind a screen in court or "supported by someone" in court.

11.7 provides for a Special Measures Review Application, Form 11E. The sheriff may vary, add, substitute or delete measures already stipulated.

11.8 applies to evidence given before the commissioner and provides that it must be video recorded. Traditionally, evidence taken on commission is not.

Expert Witness Evidence is not covered by the Simple Procedure Rules. As in the case of remit to a person of skill this is a curious omission.

In practical terms the engagement of experts is one of the most unsatisfactory areas of simple procedure or indeed of any system of low value court actions. The principal reasons are availability and cost.

Take as an example a claim that a fitted kitchen was installed shoddily and that it will cost £1000 to put it right. The best evidence is an estimate from another kitchen fitter or, preferably, two estimates from different kitchen fitters. However, the likelihood is that those fitters will be looking to gain the work from the claimant. That motivation immediately compromises their independence. If they are not independent they will fall foul of one of the key tests set out in the definitive authority on the matter, *Kennedy v Cordia* (Services) LLP, namely "whether the witness is impartial in his or her presentation and assessment of the evidence."

So to ensure independence one would be looking for an estimate from a kitchen fitter who is told in advance that he will not be getting the work and will be paid just to provide an opinion, one which might have to be followed up by him appearing in court. It is reasonable to assume that there are very few kitchen fitters who will be interested in getting involved. The same is true of car mechanics, roofers, central heating engineers and pretty well any other types of tradesmen. Generally, a plumber or electrician wants to practise his trade, not give reports on the shortcomings of other plumbers or electricians so that they can be sued successfully.

In addition, the tradesman witness has to be paid. He has to look at the workmanship of his fellow tradesman, compile a report then perhaps give up several hours of time to attend court. Including VAT he might charge the better part of £1000, especially if he knows that there is a shortage of others willing to undertake these tasks. In any simple procedure claim this kind of outlay is a major and probably an excessively disproportionate cost.

Of course, it might well be possible to have the tradesman witness certified as a skilled person (see below) but as with all third parties who have to be paid in pursuit of a claim, including the sheriff clerk, sheriff officers and witnesses in general, there is no guarantee of ever being re-imbursed by the opponent in the event of success.

Scotland is not alone in having had to struggle with these issues. Consider the Canadian provinces; to try to avoid the need for experts to attend court the British Columbian small claims system allows the party to file i.e. lodge an expert's report by serving it on other parties at least 30 days before trial. The other parties can insist on attendance but will be liable in the expenses of that witness if it proves to have been unnecessary. Similar rules apply in Yukon, Newfoundland and Labrador where the period is 14 days.

As has already been discussed, evidence will always be admissible. However, a case may then fail based on the inadequacy of that evidence. The lawyer has to minimise the risk of being blamed for that failure.

The New Zealand caselaw shows that the lack of expert evidence can be fatal. *QT v B Ltd* [2024] N.Z.D.T.148 (26th April 2024) concerned a company which carried out earthworks. These were allegedly incomplete and substandard. The evidence comprised photographs, invoices and quotes. There was an email from the council. This claim failed due to insufficient evidence. There was "anecdotal evidence of some slips ... concerns raised by a neighbour, some photos of the site and a plan". It was not enough. An expert witness might have tipped the balance, but such witnesses are expensive.

On the other hand, in *OB v CM* [2014] N.Z.D.T. 121 photographic evidence was enough. In this case, which would never be reported were it in Scotland, the applicant had bought a dog collar for the equivalent of about £34. The photographs showed fraying around the buckle, indicating that the leather was insufficiently strong. The applicant was successful.

CHAPTER EIGHTEEN

PROOF AND THE GRANTING OF DECREE

Part 12 is headed **The Hearing** and consists of 12.1 to 12.6

This Part is very short, but it is also incomplete. It fails to deal with the court's disposal of the case after the hearing; this is covered by 13.1(1) and 13.2 to 13.4.

Again, it is important to say something about the use of terms, and the problems that can arise.

The term "hearing" is used here synonymously with the diet otherwise known as "proof" under both ordinary and summary cause procedure. To an extent, one can see why that latter term was avoided, since it could be misconstrued by a party litigant as meaning evidence, i.e. material rather than an event, such as that the proof of the pudding is in the eating.

12.1 states that Part 12 is "about the hearing at which the dispute between the parties should be resolved." and 12.2 that the "purpose of the hearing is to help the sheriff to resolve the dispute". This definition has already been provided at 7.8. These definitions are meaningless. The dispute could equally well be resolved at the Case Management Discussion under 7.7.

It has already been suggested that the better definition of a hearing would be that it is "to enable evidence to be heard by the court to help the sheriff to resolve the dispute between the parties".

Instead, "evidence" is simply omitted from 12.2.

Under the Small Claims Rules 1988 and 2002 the term "hearing" was also used. It is used in England also. The format of a proof is very similar under small claims procedure in England (See CPR 27.8.) The court may adopt any method of proceeding at a hearing that it considers to be fair, hearings will be informal, the strict rules of evidence do not apply, the court need not take evidence on oath and it may limit cross-examination. This is not uncommon in other Commonwealth jurisdictions.

One deficiency of New Zealand procedure is that hearings are held in private. This is not a good idea. There are sound constitutional reasons why it is regarded as desirable for justice to be administered in public. (see for example *Scott v Scott* 1913 A.C. 417.) So there are problems with hearings "in chambers", especially where the sheriff has huge power over how to act. Publicity is seen as being conducive to accountability for the way in which judges and sheriffs conduct themselves. Article 6 refers to the right to a "public hearing". The parties may waive that right but the public interest remains. Litigation is not arbitration.

By contrast, New Zealand Judge Peter Spiller's view is that "Privacy is seen to make for a more accessible Tribunal, encourages free, open and frank exchange, allows the parties to take part in negotiation more readily, and gives the parties a safe environment in which to sort the matter out without loss of face". These remarks are due respect. It should be noted too that the lack of public access to these New Zealand proofs is offset to a degree by the fact that the decisions taken are well reported. The Scottish public can learn more about how these hearings are conducted than about those in Scotland.

Since the simple procedure rules so often Anglicise the terminology of Scottish procedure perhaps they ought to have used the word "trial" instead of hearing in Part 12. That is the term used in Ontario, for example.

Alternatively, the term "evidence hearing" would have distinguished it from the "time to pay hearing" of 5.6(2) and the "expenses hearing" of 14.5.

Far worse, however, the rules offend against the need for any set of rules of court to use terms properly and consistently across all fields of law. The simple procedure rules do not comply with this necessity; as we have seen with regards to Part 10 they refer to "evidence" in the informal sense, which creates nothing but uncertainty.

If the rules are to use the word evidence at all they should do so in the legal sense. Otherwise, they should avoid the term and deploy a legally neutral term such as "material" instead.

There is much to criticise in 12.6. It must be said, however, that the following two could have been levelled at small claims procedure too, and for the same reasons;

12.3 and 12.4 labour the point that the sheriff must encourage negotiation and A.D.R. 12.4(2) requires the sheriff to "identify the factual basis and legal basis of the claim and the response to the claim." This sounds rather like the same exercise that ought to have been conducted, and no doubt was, at the Case Management Discussion

12.5 deals with the situation where one or both parties fails to appear; in the event of the absence of one party this "may" result in dismissal – so the action can be re-raised – or a decision (i.e. decree). Where neither side appears "the sheriff must dismiss the claim". The reason for the absence of discretion in this last situation is unclear. Recall procedure is provided for by 13.5.

Assume that everyone is keen to proceed to proof, or (more likely) is resigned to doing so. 12.6(1) states that "Before evidence is heard the sheriff must explain … the way the sheriff has decided to consider evidence at the hearing". 12.6(2) empowers the sheriff to "impose conditions on how evidence is presented" and to set time limits.

One might say that if this explanation and imposition of conditions comes fifteen minutes before the evidence commences they come more than a little late given that long before this point the parties will -or certainly ought to – have prepared their respective cases, taken decisions on which productions to lodge, witness to call and submissions to make. A proof is like a battle, and the protagonists should have strategies in place well before they set foot in the arena. Giving the sheriff these powers to thwart these plans is another example of the perils of having a system which is neither fish nor fowl, neither adversarial nor inquisitorial.

To achieve justice the sheriff well may be drawn towards abandoning her non-interventionist role and wading into the fray but this is fundamentally at odds with the nature of a Scottish sheriff or judge. By all means have an interventionist presiding but that ought to happen in a tribunal and not in a court.

The hearing is likely to be the point where the solicitor's fees soar, simply because it can be so time consuming. Unless the hearing is remote there will be travelling time. The solicitor has no control over relevant factors such as waiting time at court, how long the opponent will take to examine his witnesses or to undertake cross examination or to make submissions or how long the sheriff will take or whether the hearing will be discharged. There are likely to be other hearings set down for the same time, usually at 10am. Getting started can be an achievement in itself.

12.6(3) states that "the sheriff may decide whether the evidence is to be taken on oath or affirmation or not."

Leaving aside the question of why it would ever be appropriate for an adult witness not to be expected to take the oath or to affirm this rule infers that an individual who enters a witness box and speaks is thereby giving evidence. Plainly, that is incorrect unless "evidence" is being used here colloquially. It probably is.

Only the oath or affirmation differentiates an affidavit and a precognition. Previous rules were different. Small Claim Rule 1988 16(3) stated that evidence shall be given on oath or affirmation. Small Claim Rule 2002 9.3(6) watered this down, but still maintained the expectation that this would happen. Unfortunately, they implied that an oral account could still be "evidence" even if not given on oath or affirmation. This is the only conclusion to be drawn from the rule that "Evidence will normally be taken on oath or affirmation but the sheriff may dispense with that requirement if it appears reasonable to do so." One would expect oral testimony to be given on oath or affirmation, however.

12.6(4) allows the sheriff to ask questions. 12.6(5) and (6) allows the inspection of evidence or a place as long as the parties or representatives are present. These three provisions do not innovate on conventional practice. They may well simply be designed to inform party litigants that these powers exist.

The absence of any clear rules of evidence is worse than a lack of detailed rules of procedure. The process was actually fairer and more predictable more than a century ago. At that time Section 8 of the Sheriff Courts (Scotland) Act 1907 provided that "In a summary cause the sheriff shall order such procedure as he thinks requisite and (without a record of the evidence ... shall dispose of the cause without delay." Although the section was a little sparse on procedural detail it clarified that there would in principle be evidence. The problem is that simple procedure micromanages procedure but has no rules whatsoever in relation to evidence.

To function properly and fairly any court process needs to have predictability. Otherwise, a dispute might as well be taken out of court and remitted to an individual who can decide the matter in whatever manner she or he wishes. Unfortunately, a simple procedure hearing is an unhappy mix of a contest with no rules. Parties have one chance to present their cases but do not know how they will be expected to do that.

There are problems in preparing for a proof hearing under simple procedure by reason of the fact that one cannot refer to rules, judicial practice or binding precedent. Taking these in turn;

1) The rules of normal evidence do not apply and there is nothing by way of guidance to replace them. For example, there would

appear to be nothing to stop a party lodging a precognition, letter (signed or not), email or text as a production whereupon the person precognosed or author need not attend as a witness. Clearly the weight to be attached to the item would be far lighter than to parole evidence, but neither would be inadmissible according to the rules. More serious would be the situation that would arise if, minutes before the hearing was due to start, the sheriff stated, with reference to 12.6(1) that he had decided to hear in person from that witness.

2) There is no body of reported cases on how in practice a case should be proved. The S.C.T.S. website publishes judgments but many decisions are issued orally and of the written ones, whilst Court of Session decisions are normally published those in the sheriff court will be published only if they involve a matter of principle, a particular point of general public importance or is of legal significance. As has already been observed, the vast majority of simple procedure cases do not fall into any of these categories and are never published.

3) Even if there were to be wholesale publication of simple procedure cases (as there is in New Zealand) none of these decisions is binding on anyone. Each sheriff has more or less complete control over how she wishes to decide to conduct the hearing and she could legitimately decide the next case on substantially the same facts on a different basis. Further, since each case turns on its own circumstances it is unlikely that there will ever be an authority from the appeal court on how a sheriff must manage and assess evidence. Sheriffs are generally entrusted with the process to deal with as they see fit.

From a risk management perspective how does the solicitor accommodate these problems?

As regards 1) the safe approach is to treat the hearing as if the normal rules of evidence do apply to oneself and not to the other party. A simple procedure hearing is like a game of chess where the bishops may move only diagonally unless the umpire otherwise directs. One would have to play as if one had two bishops and the opponent had three queens.

Bear in mind that the hearing will be before a legally qualified person whose background will have been in legal fields where there are rules of evidence. Accordingly, it would be advisable to recover and lodge the best evidence that can be obtained subject to time and funding restraints. Equally, objecting to the opponent's evidence (giving it that term colloquially) will probably be futile because nothing is inadmissible. "Evidence" is basically any material whatsoever, with nothing inadmissible and everything simply thrown in and weighed in the balance.

So, it would be unwise to lodge precognitions or even affidavits unless the client is made aware of the risks and possible consequences of the fact that the sheriff is bound to attach less weight to that material. Clients should be advised to call all important witnesses to attend the hearing in person.

In respect of 2) and 3) practitioners simply have to play it safe and approach the case as if it were an ordinary action.

S.C.T.S. ought to report far more written simple procedure case decisions. The lack of the application of the law of evidence makes this even more imperative.

The real solution is to take small value claims out of the sheriff court altogether, of course, and to entrust them to a New Zealand style tribunal.

Part 13 is headed **The Decision** and comprises 13.1 to 13.7. Importantly, it includes the mechanism for recall of decree.

The term "decision" is used here synonymously with "decree".

13.2(2) requires the sheriff to issue a decision within 4 weeks from the date of the proof hearing. Unlike unless orders, there are no consequences if he does not.

13.3 envisages that the sheriff will give an *ex tempore* decision immediately upon evidence having concluded or that a Decision Form 13A will be issued.

13.4 allows the sheriff to grant decree for money, delivery of property or performance of an obligation. He can grant a decision which "dismisses the claim" or "absolves [i.e assoilzies] the respondent". The latter but not the former gives rise to *res judicata*, precluding the raising of the same action. Conventionally, absolvitor is apt where evidence has been led. Otherwise dismissal would be appropriate.

13.5 is headed "When can a decision be recalled?" and is the equivalent of the recall of decree provisions in the summary cause and small claims rules. 13.5(1) states that recall is allowed where a decision is made in a party's absence. This is misleading. The decision which the respondent sought to recall in *Bell v Farmer and Farmer* [2023] SAC (Civ) 10 followed his having failed to lodge a Response Form. There was no failure to appear in the literal sense. A lawyer might understand the meaning of the phrase that a defender has figuratively "failed to enter appearance" but a party litigant respondent would probably be confused by the apparent lack of remedy against a decree granted because he did not lodge the necessary form.

If dismissal is granted "a party" – the applicant, presumably – has a fortnight to apply to recall. Otherwise, the deadline is the point at which a decision is fully implemented. A party can apply only once.

13.6 covers the Application to Recall. 13.6(2) requires that a respondent who wishes to dispute the claim must include a Response Form with the Application to Recall. 13.6 (4) requires that a diet ("a discussion in court") be assigned, making it clear, therefore, that the choice of whether to recall is discretionary. To a large extent this procedure mirrors that of reponing other than that a Reponing Note does not require to be accompanied by separate Defences.

13.7 states that if recall is granted the sheriff must give orders. Essentially this is akin to the situation where an ordinary cause defender is reponed. Once the case is back on track everyone needs to know its next destination.

CHAPTER NINETEEN

EXPENSES

Part 14 is headed **Expenses,** consists of 14.1 to 14.5 and is probably the most badly drafted Part of all. That is unfortunate given the importance of the subject matter. Expenses are a major factor in why solicitors need to be extraordinarily careful in acting in simple procedure.

An area which causes clients confusion and consternation is the discrepancy between the amount that they have to pay their own lawyer – which is governed by the terms of engagement- and the amount that they are allowed to recover in expenses from their opponent, a matter determined by the Table of Fees. Many question why they have been left out of pocket at all when they have been entirely successful in a court action. The system can leave lawyers exposed. To the client it can look as if the solicitor is overcharging. The Table of Fees is too low, of course.

Simple procedure clients need to be warned, at the outset and at frequent intervals, that they are going to be out of pocket, win or lose and that advice needs to be evidenced by email, letter or file note.

Part 14 is incomplete (which is why it is so short), it uses misleading language and it is likely to baffle anyone who is not legally qualified.

14.2(1) provides that "Once a claim has been resolved, the sheriff must make an order about expenses, such as (a) that no payments are to be made in respect of the expenses of any party, (b) that a payment is to be made to a party or to a party's solicitor." This differentiation between the party and agent may relate to the notion of the latter as agent disburser, whereby the court can bypass the client and allow the agent to recover expenses in his own name. Whether to do so is a matter entirely for the discretion of the sheriff (*Dobie*, p329). The author has seen this done on only a couple of occasions. Small Claim Rule 21.6(15) allowed the court to grant a decree for expenses in favour of a solicitor.

14.2(2) states that expenses regarding "a courtroom supporter may not be part of an order about expenses."

14.3(1) explains that "where the expenses of a claim are capped, the sheriff must make an order about expenses when deciding the claim." Otherwise, (2) where expenses are uncapped an order must be made, if possible, "when deciding the claim" or (3) where that is impossible, "after deciding the claim."

14.3(2) seems entirely unrealistic, since uncapped expenses entail that an account be produced. The winner will not have enough time to produce an account and the sheriff is not qualified to scrutinise it; that is the job of the sheriff clerk acting as auditor.

14.4 provides that if 14.3(3) applies the sheriff must not send out a Decision Form until an expenses order is made but in terms of 14.4(2) and (3) must give written orders which arrange an expenses hearing.

This is roundabout way of stating the obvious, that a final decree may not be granted until expenses have been determined.

14.4(4) states that the successful party must (prior to amendment of this rule in 2022 the word was "may") send an account of expenses before the expenses hearing. Under 14.4(5) the sheriff clerk may be required "to assess the level of expenses" and to send "notice of that assessment to the parties before the expenses hearing." At this diet the sheriff must make an order.

14.4 is far too restrictive. It does not appear to allow the sheriff to decide the merits of a case and to go away and ponder the issue of expenses, even overnight, after having heard a whole day's evidence, without compelling him to require that an account of expenses be lodged. That might be entirely pointless if the disposal of expenses is that there be none.

14.5 asks "What is an expenses hearing?" and then replies that it is" to assess the level of expenses (if any) that should be awarded to a party" The sheriff must make an order akin to those at 14.2 (1) (a) and (b).

The phrase "level of expenses" is misleading. This term customarily indicates not a figure but the scale which it is appropriate to apply to an account in order to reach a figure. For example, this could be the Summary Cause scale. 14.4(5) and 14.5(1) should omit the words "level of"; they are pointless, unnecessary and confusing.

As already mentioned, amongst other faults this Part is incomplete. In particular, it fails to mention three key pieces of legislation which are essential reading;

1. The Courts Reform (Scotland) Act 2014 Section 81 which is headed "Expenses in simple procedure cases"

2. The Sheriff Court Simple Procedure (Limits on Awards of Expenses) Order 2016 and

3. The Act of Sederunt (Taxation of Judicial Expenses Rules) 2019 No. 75

Incidentally, expenses in those simple procedure cases commenced before 29th April 2019 were subject not to the 2019 Rules but to the Act of Sederunt (Fees of Solicitors in the Sheriff Court) (Amendment and Further Provisions) 1993. In particular, Chapter V, "Simple Procedure" had a Part 1 for Admitted Claims and Part 2 for Disputed Claims. The former's Inclusive Fee for all work, including taking instructions up to applying for a decision was only £223.80, the equivalent of about an hour's work. It is hard to conceive that a solicitor would charge less than this, leaving the client with a shortfall between his own solicitor's fee and this figure.

For the party litigant there is little point in Part 14 referring to expenses being "capped" when there is no explanation there as to its meaning. It is absent from the Glossary too. Instead, one has to conduct some research, looking firstly at Regulation 3(1); "a case where the expenses are capped" means a simple procedure case … to which an order made under section 81(1) of the Courts Reform (Scotland) Act 2014 applies". Thereafter, one has to look at that section and the secondary legislation linked to it, namely The Sheriff Court Simple Procedure (Limits on Awards of Expenses) Order 2016.

Regulation 2 of the 2016 Order, as amended, provides that no award of expenses is to be made where the value of the claim is less than or equal to £300, and Regulation 3 imposes caps on awards up to and including £3000. (see below).

S81(5)(a)(ii) of the 2014 Act provides that the cap does not apply where a defender has stated a defence but has not proceeded with it. This is an interesting issue and one that has never been satisfactorily resolved.

Jamie Davis v Skyfire Insurance [2019] SC EDIN 24 exemplifies the irony of removing protection against heavy expenses from a party who wants to settle a claim once the action has become defended. This was a problem under small claims procedure too; it sometimes made economic sense to take a futile case to proof and lose rather than doing the otherwise sensible thing of throwing in the towel before that stage was reached. The expenses would be less as long as the court did not deem that the loser had acted unreasonably in going ahead. In the case mentioned liability was admitted but *quantum* was not. The claim was for £3035 but it settled for £1700 on the eve of the hearing. The sheriff found that the respondent had not proceeded with his defence so that the cap did not apply. That was undeniable. However, the sheriff also noted that parties should be encouraged to settle by negotiation at any stage of an action. He observed that "it cannot make sense …to punish a party who avoids a hearing, and who … is at least partially ... successful ... and who negotiates a settlement without taking up court and parties' time and resources with a hearing."

In taking this approach the sheriff was following principle 4 of 1.2, that "Parties are to be encouraged to settle ... and should be able to do so throughout the progress of a case." Penalising them for doing so even the day before the hearing is hardly very encouraging.

Of course, even without a cap the question of expenses is within the court's discretion and in *Davis* the sheriff very wisely awarded a sum in expenses which was the equivalent capped amount. This was £170 instead of the thousands which would have been brought out in an uncapped account. £170 was 10% of the value of the action, the percentage payable having regard to the 2016 Order for claims worth between £1500 and £3000.

Other sheriff courts have not followed this benign approach. See, for example *Ian Graham v Paul Farrell* [2017] SC EDIN 75, a case in which a Tender was lodged and accepted.

This lack of consistency between sheriffs, and the absence of a determination by the Sheriff Appeal Court, is not helpful to the practitioner trying to advise either party. The respondent does not know how much he might have to pay if his Tender is accepted and the claimant does not know how much he will receive if he takes it. All the lawyer can do is advise the client of the law, warn about the risks and let the client take the decision.

Of course, as has already been mentioned, Tenders are not governed or even referred to in the Simple Procedure Rules.

S81(5)(b) of the 2014 Act provides another scenario where the cap will not apply, i.e. where the losing party has acted in a manner which is "manifestly unreasonable". This could include carrying on with a desperately feeble case. Incidentally, the word "manifestly", was inserted by section 12 of the Civil Litigation (Expenses and Group Proceedings) (Scotland) Act 2018, thereby enhancing the loser's protection against the risk of liability for uncapped expenses. The term "manifestly unreasonable" is analysed in Lady Justice Arden in *Dransfield and another v Information Commissioner* (2016) 3 All E.R. 221.

The term used under small claim procedure was "unreasonable conduct". In *Milne v Uniroyal Englebert Tyres Ltd* 1995 SLT (Sh Ct) 23 the case had gone to proof, and the sheriff had preferred the defender's evidence. The latter sought unrestricted expenses. On appeal, Sheriff Principal Nicolson thought that it was "necessary to come close to the position of being able to say that he [the pursuer] has knowingly put forward a false case" to be guilty of unreasonable conduct.

In reality, the process of getting to a figure of expenses is easy. Someone ought to devise a flowchart. These are the steps;

1. The sheriff decides who is entitled to the expenses.
2. If those expenses are *prima facie* capped by Section 81 of the 2014 Act the sheriff has to decide whether to disapply the cap or not.
3. If he does not disapply it he quantifies expenses there and then by reference to the 2016 Act of Sederunt.
4. If he does disapply it, or if the expenses are uncapped by Section 81, he passes the matter to the sheriff clerk and invites the successful party to lodge an account which is compiled by that party with reference to the 2019 Act of Sederunt.
5. Thereafter, the sheriff clerk conducts a diet to scrutinise the account and hear objections to it by the other party.
6. The sheriff clerk then reaches a figure and reports this to the sheriff.
7. The sheriff then approves that figure unless a party objects to it in which case he will hear and determine those objections at a diet before approving the figure.

One would never discern this from Part 14. In particular, it fails to mention the diet referred to at 5) of this list. There are essentially three "expenses diets", at 1), 5) and 7) in this list. 14.5 refers only to 7).

Party litigants must find the process unfathomable. For a start, it will be a shock to realise that the task falls to them to frame an account. They would have no reason to know anything about the 2019 Act of Sederunt without which knowledge they would be unable to compile accounts. In addition, the title of that enactment is misleading to most, who will assume, quite understandably, that Taxation of Judicial Expenses means applying tax. In fact, there is a mention of tax in the Act of Sederunt (VAT to be exact) but lawyers know that "taxing" an account of expenses in the context of this Act of Sederunt means scrutinising and challenging it. The term is used in Commonwealth jurisdictions including Australia and Nova Scotia.

Rule 3.3, headed "Table of charges" provides at paragraphs (1) and (2) that for ordinary causes the solicitor has the choice of framing the account on the basis of detailed charges found in Schedule 1 or block fees contained in a table of inclusive charges. By contrast, paragraph (4) states that subject to Rule 3.7 ("Simple procedure") the charges to be allowed in respect of a simple procedure case ... are those specified in the applicable table of inclusive charges in schedule 5."

So it is not competent to frame a simple procedure account of expenses with reference to the detailed charges found in Schedule 1. Instead, only the "applicable table of inclusive charges" must be used. This is all subject to the caveat in Rule 3.3(5); "This rule – i.e. Rule 3.3 – applies unless the court otherwise directs."

Schedule 5 is headed "Tables of Inclusive Charges for Simple Procedure Cases" and there are only two, the first Table being headed "Admitted Claims" and the other being headed "Disputed Claims".

There is also Schedule 3. Table of Inclusive Charges for Work Undertaken by Solicitors in the Sheriff Appeal Court under the Act of

Sederunt (Sheriff Appeal Court Rules) 2015; in which there is to be found Table 3, Appeals from Simple Procedure Cases.

If the expenses are capped (by the 2016 Act of Sederunt) there are essentially three bands into which the case must fall;

- If the award is equal to or less than £300 no expenses are payable. Before 2019 this figure was £200.

- From £300.01 to £1500 the expenses are limited to £150.

- From £1500.01 to £3000 the expenses are limited to 10% of the award.

As regards the cap, in *Sloan v Mycock 1992 SLT (Sh Ct) 23* the court held that where there were several defenders in an unsuccessful small claims action the maximum payable (which at that time was £75) was an aggregate, i.e it was not £75 per defender.

Part 14 and indeed the 2016 Act of Sederunt are silent as to whether these capped figures are inclusive or exclusive of outlays including the sum that the claimant has had to pay the sheriff clerk in order to raise the action.

This omission is all the worse given that confusion existed on this very point under small claims procedure too. The opportunity was there to clarify the matter but, alas, it was not taken. There is currently conflicting case law on the point and none of the cases are binding anyway given that they are all sheriff court decisions.

The outlays may be small but relative to the capped amounts they are significant.

In *Natalie Gowans v Elizabeth Miller* [2017] SC FOR 82 the sheriff took the view that the capped award of expenses was all inclusive, i.e. it encompassed the solicitor's fees and VAT and the warranting fee.

Accordingly, the court awarded the pursuer £218.45 (10% of the value of the claim) inclusive of VAT and outlays. Around half that award will have been for the sheriff clerk's warranting fee alone.

On the other hand, in *Ashleigh Potter v OSC Group Ltd* unreported 12th July 2017 Aberdeen Sheriff Court – from *Macphail* 4th edition [1st September 2021] the sheriff took the approach that the 1993 Act of Sederunt referred to "work done and expenses or outlays incurred" whereas both that of 2016, and the 2014 Act refer only to expenses. If the intention had been to exclude VAT and outlays that would have been made clear. So the sheriff allowed VAT and outlays to be included. The court followed this same approach in *Andrew Martin v Southern Rock Insurance Co Ltd* [2018] SC EDIN and allowed outlays and VAT in addition to the £150 expenses that the parties had agreed as part of their settlement contract.

However, as can be seen, there is no binding authority or consistency of shrieval opinion on the matter. Accordingly, clients have to be warned that the topic is unpredictable.

Anything above £3000 is not affected by the 2016 Act of Sederunt and is therefore uncapped.

The following is a style account which was prepared in relation to a breach of missives simple procedure case in Ayr Sheriff Court and in which absolvitor was granted following a hearing of evidence. The sum sued for was £5000. The account was lodged and was approved by the auditor of South Strathclyde, Dumfries and Galloway in its entirely, with no abatements. It is typical of how such accounts bring out figures comparable to, if not more than, the sum sued for.

ACCOUNT OF EXPENSES FOR THE RESPONDENTS

In terms of the Act of Sederunt (Taxation of Judicial Expenses Rules) 2019 No.75 as amended

Schedule 5 Table 2; Disputed Claims

1.	Before the simple procedure case begins; correspondence with claimants and their agents over the dispute	15 units	£270.00
2.(b)	Taking instructions, considering Claim Form and preparing a Response Form	15 units	£270.00
4.(a)	Preparation for and attendance at case management discussion on 4 November 2024	15 units	£270.00
(b)	Continued case management discussion on 16 December 2024	20 mins	£72.00
(c)	10 February 2025 pre-Proof Hearing	15 mins	£54.00
5.	<u>Precognitions:</u> Precognition of Mr Bagot (respondent) Precognitions of Mr Green	2 pages 6 pages	£180.00 £540.00
6.	Application (b) considering claimant's application to amend Statement of Claim	5 units	£90.00
8.(a)	Preparation for Hearing	32.5 units	£585.00
(d)	Inspecting opponent's documents	2 hours	£360.00

	Hearing 10.00 am to 12.45 pm and 2.15 pm to 3.00 pm	35 units	£630.00
	Settlement (b) offer of settlement made 30 November 2023 and subsequent correspondence	17.5 units	£315.00
12.	Account of Expenses	10 units	£180.00
			£3816.00
		Less 10%	£381.60
			£3434.40
		VAT	£686.88
		TOTAL	**£4121.28**

Relevant provisions of the 2019 Rules (which are divided into paragraphs);

The hourly rate of charge;

Rule 3.2; 1 unit equates to £18 (£16.40 for work undertaken before 30th June 2023). This is a starting point.

This is the same figure whether a case be in the sheriff court, Sheriff Appeal Court or indeed in the Court of Session. However, in simple procedure, the figure is in effect modified to a lower amount due to the abatements required by Rule 3.7(3). See below.

Rule 3.3(4); subject to Rule 3.7 (simple procedure), the charges to be allowed in respect of a simple procedure in the sheriff court are those specified in the applicable tables of inclusive charges in schedule 5. There is no option to compile an account by listing particular items of work, or using "time and line" as it is known. There are two tables, for Admitted Claims and Disputed Claims.

Rule 3.3(5) provides that Rule 3.3 applies unless the court otherwise directs. This power given to the court reflects the fact that the sheriff retains considerable discretion over expenses.

Rule 3.7 (2); All charges allowed by the Auditor are to be reduced by 10%. Accordingly, the unit becomes only £16.20. It may then be reduced *further*;

Rule 3.7(3) Unless the court otherwise directs, where the total value of the claim is £2500 or less, all charges allowed by the Auditor, as already reduced in accordance with paragraph (2), are to be further reduced –

a. Where the total value of the claim is less than £1000, by 50%

b. Otherwise by 25%

So there are essentially three bands; remember too that these are uncapped expenses;

- 1p to £999; the unit value is a meagre £8.10.
- £1000 to £2499.99; a marginally better unit value of £12.15.
- £2500 to £5000; an improved but still inadequate unit value of £16.20.

Note that if a claim is relatively small within simple procedure an award of uncapped expenses will yield a very meagre sum given that one is compelled to use the table of block fees rather than detailed charges and that the account must be reduced considerably.

Rule 5.1 relates to three distinct methods of increasing the costs recoverable by the winner from the loser. All three apply to all types of action in the sheriff court, and in the Sheriff Appeal Court. Significantly, they all apply in simple procedure. Taking them in turn;

<u>Application by a party for an additional charge</u>

Rule 5.2(3) states that the court "must grant the application when satisfied that an increase is justified to reflect the responsibility undertaken by the solicitor in the conduct of the proceedings."

Rule 5.2(3) requires that if the application is granted the sheriff must "specify a percentage increase in the charges to be allowed at taxation." Since "taxation" is not a word used in simple procedure there requires to be some translation. This exercise leads one to conclude that the application has to be made before the conclusion of the "expenses hearing" as it is called in Simple Procedure Rule 14.5. The percentage increase must pre-date or at least precede the outcome of the diet of assessment undertaken by the sheriff clerk, i.e the taxation of expenses.

Rule 5.1(2) requires that under simple procedure the application be made "by incidental (sic.) orders application." This can only be a reference to an "additional" orders application under Part 9 of the Simple Procedure Rules. This applies to skilled witness and sanction for counsel applications too.

Rule 5.2 directs the sheriff to have regard to a variety of factors including complexity and novelty and the number and importance of documents etc. These are listed under seven headings. Militating against an increase is...

> "(f) the amount or value of money or property involved in the proceedings."

Having regard to proportionality, this reflects the pragmatic reality that small value claims should not really merit large fees.

Skilled Persons (commonly known as Expert Witnesses)

The two relevant Rules are; Skilled persons; Rule 4.5 and Certification of skilled person; Rule 5.3.

These two rules concern that which is commonly but erroneously known as the "expert witness". The correct term is "skilled person". A person is "skilled" only if the court certifies that he is. Certification has to be sought by "a party" though it is hard to envisage why that party would ever be anyone other than the party who engaged the person. The test for certification is that the person is skilled and that it is, or was, reasonable and proportionate to employ him. The requirement for proportionality is an interesting one in the context of a low value action. Nevertheless, there is no doubt that both these rules apply to simple procedure. It is specifically mentioned in Rule 4.5(4)(a)(iii) and Rule 5.3(4)(c) which disapply Rule 4.5(1)(b) and Rule 5.3(5) respectively. These latter rules require that an application for certification be made prospectively unless with cause shown for why the application is made after the work has been undertaken. Accordingly, simple procedure is more lenient than, for example, ordinary cause procedure in terms of the timing of an application for certification of a skilled person.

If certification is granted under Rule 5.3 then Rule 4.5 is engaged and the party is entitled to seek recovery in his account of expenses of the charge incurred by him to the person who has been "engaged for the ... application of that person's skill". The charge is treated as an outlay in the account.

Sanction for the employment of counsel; Rule 5.4

Simple procedure is meant to be conducted in such a way that solicitors are unnecessary. *A fortiori*, it ought not to require the involvement of an advocate. The maximum value of the claim is only £5000. Counsel's fees are bound to be a sizeable chunk of that.

Sanction may be sought, however. This process is similar to the certification of skilled persons insofar as it is one thing for the client to pay for the assistance of expert reports and testimony and for the representation of an advocate, quite another for the opponent to pick up the bill.

As with certification of a skilled person, simple procedure is specifically mentioned in Rule 5.4 (4)(b) which has the effect of disapplying Rule 5.4(5) and (6). These latter rules require that an application for sanction be made prospectively unless with cause shown for why the application is made after the work has been undertaken. Again, therefore, simple procedure is comparably lenient in terms of the timing of an application for sanction for counsel.

The sheriff may sanction the whole action, part of the action, some of the work or a combination thereof as suitable for the employment of counsel; Rule 5.4(2).

Rule 5.4(3) makes it clear that sanction may be granted for junior or senior counsel or for more than one counsel, though it is hard to envisage that ever happening in a simple procedure case. Instead, such a case would likely be transferred to ordinary cause procedure under 17.2.

Unlike the comparable provisions relative to skilled persons, however, there is no test within the 2019 Rules to determine when sanction should be granted. Instead, the test is to be found in primary legislation, namely section 108 of the 2014 Act.

This provides at S108(2) that the "court must sanction the employment of counsel if the court considers, in all the circumstances of the case, that it is reasonable to do so." Specific direction is made to the difficulty or complexity of the proceedings and "the importance or value of any claim in the proceedings". Also, the court is to have regard to "the desirability of ensuring that no party gains an unfair advantage by virtue of the employment of counsel." This last factor raises the issue known as "equality of arms".

The "value of the claim" is in essence a proportionality test. Again, this highly significant in low value actions. The Personal Injury Court case of *Ackrim v UK Insurance Ltd* [2024] SC EDIN 53 concerned a rear shunt whiplash car accident in which the sheriff assessed damages at a mere £3144, yet counsel was instructed for both sides. The sheriff's decision of 5th December 2024 reserved the question of expenses.

CHAPTER TWENTY

ENFORCING A DECREE IN SCOTLAND

Part 15 is ambitiously headed **How to enforce a decision** and consists of 15.1 to 15.5. This concerns diligence in execution and it is the stage at which the client learns whether the process has been worth it. If he decides not, the solicitor has to have taken all necessary precautions to ensure that he will not be blamed. Interim diligence is governed by Part 20.

The heading ought to have the suffix "in Scotland" because that is the extent of it.

15.2(1) requires the successful party to "wait 4 weeks before enforcing a decision". This is because the loser has 4 weeks to appeal; 16.2(1). The rest of 15.2 explains that a decision under appeal or recall or one that has been recalled must not be enforced.

15.3 (2) to (8) relates to three distinct forms of diligence, namely an earnings arrestment, an attachment (of goods) and a money attachment. 15.3(2) makes clear that is a prerequisite of resorting to any of these three methods that a charge be served, a step that can be carried out only by a sheriff officer (or a solicitor if no sheriff officer is available; reference is made to the Execution of Diligence (Scotland) Act 1926, which permits this.) The days of charge are 14 days if the debtor is in the U.K. If he is not, or his address is unknown, 28 days must be given by the charge; 15.3(4).

15.3(5) states that if the charge is not complied with the creditor is entitled to instruct a sheriff officer to take the aforementioned steps of diligence. 15.4 deals with a debtor whose whereabouts are unknown.

Notable by its absence is the diligence known as land attachment. Although there is provision for this in Chapter 2 of the Bankruptcy and Diligence (Scotland) Act 2007 the Scottish Government has never brought it into effect. By contrast, in Ontario and Manitoba land attachment is an option under the small claim system.

These provisions of the rules are of course a necessity in providing a route down which the successful claimant may travel in the hope of finding a pot of gold at the end of the journey. The sad truth, of course, is that all too often the road is rocky and its destination barren. To add bitterness to the journey the traveller must pay good money in pursuit of what frequently turns out to be bad. The author has never met a sheriff officer who operates either on a "no win no fee" basis or on a "pay when paid" principle. They have their own bills to pay, as do the rest of us.

15.5 is one of the strangest rules, simply because it is linked with a form, 15B, that makes no sense. It applies where a debtor fails to comply with a decree *ad factum praestandum* or for delivery of moveables in which "the sheriff alternatively ordered the respondent to pay the claimant a sum of money."

In an ordinary cause the decree would be to ordain the defender to, for example, implement missives by conveying a disposition within 28 days of intimation which failing to pay £15,000. Or, it might be to deliver a BMW 520 with registration number SD7 NR8 within 14 days of intimation failing which to pay £15,000.

The structure of such a decree is that there is a principal remedy and that it is only if it cannot be realised (because the debtor fails to hand over the disposition or BMW) that the alternative is triggered. Importantly, there is no need for the creditor to go back to court to ask for permission to seek implementation of the alternative; indeed, the court is probably *functus* as soon as the extract is issued.

The position is completely different under simple procedure, as it was under small claims procedure. Following an unsuccessful attempt to implement the primary element of the decree the creditor cannot opt for the alternative without the permission of the court. Possibly, this is a precaution to stop dastardly creditors retrieving items but then demanding payment too.

Permission is sought by the creditor sending an Alternative Decision Application to the court. This is in Form 15B.

Form 15B states that it can be used when the sheriff has made a decision ordering the delivery of something or ordering the respondent to do something for the claimant. It professes with bewildering illogicality, that "If the court alternatively ordered the respondent to pay the claimant a sum of money, then this application can be used to ask the court to make that order."

The wording here is bizarre; if the court has made an order for payment one has to ask how it can it do so again. The form asks "What alternative order should be made?" and "Why should this order be made?"

It can only be assumed that what is envisaged is that the court will grant an order *ad factum praestandum* or delivery alone, leaving the alternative hanging, and that the case is in effect left open, giving the claimant the chance to have the decree implemented and, if it cannot be, offering him the means, i.e an Alternative Decision Application, to revert to court to obtain an enforceable order for payment.

This is how matters were under small claims procedure; Rule 41 of the 1988 Rules provided that where a decree had been granted for delivery of movables or implementation of an obligation, but the defender had not complied with it, the pursuer could "lodge with the sheriff clerk an application for decree in the alternative crave for payment." At least that was comprehensible; 15.5 is not.

Incidentally, extraneous to the Rules, Regulation 4(2) applies in actions for delivery. It states that the sheriff may grant a warrant to search for and to take possession of property and to open shut and lockfast places.

Without restrictions this clearly has the potential to affect third parties, so Reg 4(2) stipulates that the warrant applies only to premises occupied by the respondent. So if the latter transfers a motorbike to the lock up garage of his grandmother it will be put beyond the reach of this warrant.

The simple procedure rules are silent on how to enforce a simple procedure decision anywhere beyond Scotland. As regards the rest of Great Britain the answer lies in the Civil Jurisdiction and Judgments Act 1982. Section 18 and Schedules 6 and 7 prescribe the procedure. Broadly, one obtains a certificate from the sheriff court and this is then registered at the High Court in the Strand, Westminster. The fee payable to the sheriff clerk is £32 as from 1st November 2024.

Lastly, something must be said about sequestration and insolvency. Technically these are not forms of diligence but declarators of status, but in practice the threat of bankruptcy can be an effective weapon in the otherwise often feeble arsenal of the creditor. If a company debtor owes at least £750 or an individual £5000 these options are open. These sums can be the aggregate of a principal sum, expenses and interest, so simple procedure decisions are bound to fit the bill at the time that they are granted or eventually; interest continues to accumulate indefinitely, at the judicial rate of 8% *per annum*.

CHAPTER TWENTY-ONE

APPEALS

Part 16 is headed **How to appeal a decision** and consists of 16.1 to 16.4.

Practitioners need to cover their backs. The client who loses must be advised without delay that there is a right of appeal and that there is a strict time limit of 4 weeks for lodging one. In the meantime, 15.2(1) prevents the winner from enforcing the decree. The solicitor must give advice on whether she believes that an appeal is stateable. The client's instructions then need to be ascertained. This all has to be recorded and completed in time to allow any appeal to be lodged timeously.

The sheriff's treatment of expenses is a matter of discretion and the appeal courts are therefore extremely reluctant to interfere; *Douglas v Douglas* [2020] SAC (Civ) 14. This is important given the significance of expenses in proportion to the value of a simple procedure case. In addition, even if one were to fashion it into a point of law the appeal court rarely interferes with the sheriff's assessment of credibility or reliability.

Sometimes a client, stung by indignation, will wish to appeal, against the agent's advice. One option is to withdraw from acting in time for the client to obtain alternative representation. If there is insufficient time to allow fresh agents or the client himself to take up the reins, which may well be the case, it may be necessary to compile and lodge an appeal and then to withdraw. It is better to lodge a scant appeal which could be expanded later than none at all. If there is a possibility that the client will be critical of his representation at the proof there is a conflict of interest which requires the original solicitor to withdraw.

In any event, the most important immediate concern is that the four weeks do not elapse without an appeal being lodged. If that happens and the client has not stated that he did not want to appeal there is a good chance that he will complain to the S.L.C.C. that thanks to his incompetent lawyer he was deprived of his golden opportunity to lodge an appeal that had a cast iron prospect of success. The merits of the hypothetical appeal may then be the subject an argument between an experienced solicitor and a case handler who has never conducted a case in his life. Such is the reality of the current complaints and regulatory system. Practitioners must do their utmost to avoid such a scenario.

Part 16 details the requirements made of the appellant, the sheriff court and the Sheriff Appeal Court in that order. In essence, the process is not greatly different from that under the previous system other than that it is form based. 16.2, 16.3 and 16.4 state that the appellant lodges an appeal – an "Appeal Form 16A" – on points of law only, the sheriff drafts a Stated Case (here called an "Appeal Report") it is adjusted with the parties' involvement, the final Appeal Report goes to the appeal court and it answers those points and issues a determination. It can amend the Decision Form or issue a new one.

The complication that prevails and which was absent from the previous system lies in the fact that when the 2014 Act created the Sheriff Appeal Court it opened the door to secondary legislation which introduced a vast apparatus of rules, deadlines and requirements none of which existed when the appeal court consisted of the sheriff principal alone. Under Small Claim Rule 29 the appellant lodged a Note of Appeal within 14 days of final decree. The Note requested a Stated Case and specified the point of law being raised. The sheriff had 14 days to draft a Stated Case, this was adjusted with parties' involvement and the final Stated Case was sent to the sheriff principal who would then deal with the appeal at a hearing. That was truly simple procedure.

Of course, the Sheriff Appeal Court is larger and more powerful than was the Sheriff Principal. The latter's decisions were binding only within his own sheriffdom; the former's decisions are binding across Scotland in the same way as are Inner House decisions. Both those courts ordinarily comprise a bench of three which sits in a courtroom in Parliament House, Edinburgh.

Accordingly, as regards simple procedure the task of the legislators was to reconcile the complexities and cost of the Sheriff Appeal Court with the desire to keep procedure speedy, informal and inexpensive.

The solution has been to bypass some of the requirements in the Sheriff Court Appeal Rules 2021, and if possible to have the case heard by one Appeal Sheriff rather than three.

The statutory bases for an appeal from Simple Procedure are sections 82 ("Appeals from simple procedure cases") and 110 ("Appeal from a sheriff to the Sheriff Appeal Court") of the 2014 Act. Taken in conjunction these state that in simple procedure an appeal lies to that court. There is little mention of the Court of Session unlike the Summary Cause Rules which, as originally enacted, allowed the sheriff principal to certify that a case was suitable to be determined there.

As with Part 14, many party litigants are bound to struggle with appeals. For a start, it needs legal experience and knowledge to frame questions in law which do not stray into arguments about the facts. Also, questions in law need to raise the correct issues and tests. For example, there is a difference between an unreasonable exercise of discretion as opposed to a sheriff taking irrelevant factors into account or leaving relevant ones out of account. However, the distinctions may be subtle. The appellant finds no guidance about this art of pleading either in part 16 or in Form 16A. The form merely expects the appellant to state "points of law" without explaining the meaning of that term.

As with other Parts of the 2016 Rules some legitimate questions can be answered only by looking outside the Rules altogether. For instance, one might ask whether an appeal lies on interim matters (such as the refusal to grant a specification of documents) while the case is pending or only on a final decree. The Rules themselves are not explicit about this. However, the answer is clear if one looks at section 82 of the 2014 Act.

Headed "Appeals from Simple Procedure cases" it states that an appeal may be made on a point of law "against a decision of the sheriff constituting final judgment" and that "Any other decision ... is not subject to review."

Note the discrepancy between section 82 and the Simple Procedure Rules as the meaning of "decision." Section 82 clearly envisages decisions that are not final. Rule 16.1 states that "This part is about how party can appeal a decision and how the sheriff and Sheriff Appeal Court will deal with an appeal." "Decision" here means final decree, but there is nothing about finality in Part 16. It ought to be clearer, to assist party litigants and to avoid the need to look at the primary legislation underpinning the Rules.

Instead, on its own 16.2 itself merely implies that only final judgments are appealable. 16.2(1) contains the all-important provision regarding the time limit of 4 weeks after the Decision Form is sent out. Note that the meter starts to run as soon as the sheriff clerk sends that Form and not from the date of the document itself or on which it is received. That could be relevant if a judgment is dispatched just before Christmas but is seen just after New Year's Day.

Under 16.2 the appeal is made by sending an Appeal Form to the court and sending a copy to the other parties. The Appeal Form (Form 16A) must set out the legal points that the "party making the appeal" i.e the appellant, wants the Sheriff Appeal Court to answer.

16.3 relates to the sheriff's responsibilities. She must;

(1) prepare a draft Appeal Report within 4 weeks. This is the type of deadline which is largely a token exercise. Summary Cause Rule 25.1(3) provides for a time limit of 28 days. However, there is no sanction for a breach other than perhaps an awkward but gentle rebuke by the Sheriff Appeal Court. Stipulating a time limit on a sheriff is essentially an imposition of an expectation, nothing more.

(2) the Report "must set out the factual and legal basis for the decision".

(3) it "must set out legal questions for the Sheriff Appeal Court to answer."

(4) the sheriff clerk sends that draft to all the parties

(5) they have two weeks in which to add to the draft or query it

(6)–(9) the sheriff is allowed to assign a hearing on this exercise and to amend the draft

(10) the sheriff clerk sends the Sheriff Appeal Court the finalised Appeal Report together with other relevant documents.

16.3 was the subject of analysis in *Smith v Duncan* [2022] SAC (Civ) 16, a case about a dog named Martha. The appeal court was clearly of the view that the much vaunted informality of Simple Procedure does not extend to how the Appeal report is constructed.

16.4 asks what the Sheriff Appeal Court does with the appeal. It provides that;

(1) the clerk to that court must within 2 weeks arrange an appeal hearing

(2) this must be before one Appeal Sheriff unless the court otherwise directs. To practitioners, this diet will feel the same as having appeared before the Sheriff Principal under the pre-2014 Act system.

(3) to (7) require that the Appeal Sheriff/s must issue a decision immediately after the appeal hearing or within 4 weeks of it. Again, there is no sanction for a breach. This is not an "unless order" with adverse consequences to follow at the instance of the President of the Court, the Lord President or anyone else.

Reasons must be given, and the court may either amend the sheriff's Decision Form or issue a new one.

(8) states that Parts 2, 4, 5 and 6 of the Act of Sederunt Sheriff Court Appeal Rules 2021 (2021/468) apply to the appeal. Part 6 is headed "Incidental Procedure; Special Procedures."

The Sheriff Appeal Court Fees Order 2024 sets out the charges levied by the clerk to the Sheriff Appeal Court. These are exactly the same for a Simple Procedure appeal as for any other type; As of 1st November 2024 these are £67 to lodge an appeal and £283 for each day of hearing before a single Appeal Sheriff or £706 before a bench of three. Appealing in a simple procedure case is therefore disproportionately expensive compared to, for example, an ordinary cause. This uniformity of charge across each level in the sheriff court also illustrates the point, already made, that the cost of the courts' time is the same whether the action be worth £500 or £500,000. There is also no doubt the fear that if low value claims could be appealed at corresponding low charges there would be far more of them than as at present, consuming the resources of the Sheriff Appeal Court.

If the respondent appeals she will become the "respondent and appellant" whereas her opponent will be the "applicant and respondent". In other words, they will both be respondents of sorts. If the applicant appeals he will become the "applicant and appellant" whereas his opponent will be the "respondent and respondent", or maybe just "respondent". Without wishing to labour the point, simple procedure really ought to have just retained the terms pursuer and defender.

CHAPTER TWENTY-TWO

TRANSFER OF CAUSES OUT OF SIMPLE PROCEDURE, REFERENCE TO THE E.C.J, INTERVENTIONS BY THE E.H.R.C. AND S.C.H.R, DAMAGES MANAGEMENT ORDERS, CHILD'S PROPERTY ADMINISTRATION ORDERS, EQUALITY ACT 2010 CLAIMS

Part 17 is vaguely entitled **Miscellaneous Matters** and comprises 17.1 to 17.17

This Part is a medley of unrelated issues. There are six relative forms, Forms 17A to 17F.

17.2 asks how a case can be transferred out of simple procedure. It then regulates the procedure if the sheriff decides to transfer the action to the ordinary court, including the Sheriff Personal Injury Court. The claimant must lodge an initial writ and the respondent must lodge defences. The rule does not mention that that the parties will henceforth be known as pursuer and defender. 17.2 does not mention section 80 of the 2014 Act which is headed "Transfer of cases from simple procedure". This entitles a party to apply to have the case transferred and is clearly the foundation for 17.2. Neither section 20 nor 17.2 provide any guidance on when transfer would be appropriate, but the matter is obviously discretionary and will involve considerations of importance, novelty or complexity. Neither do they provide for any destination other than the ordinary roll although it is definitely not the only option; 17.15 allows a transfer to the Employment Tribunal.

A proposed amendment of the sum sued for to more than £5000 would, if granted, necessitate a remit. This happened in *Peter Cusack Property Consultancy Ltd v Simpson and others* [2024] SC GLA 44. ("The pleadings are poor on both sides but tolerably intelligible" opined the sheriff).

By contrast, Small Claim Rule 15.2 governed remits from that roll to both the summary cause and the ordinary cause roll. Does the failure of the Simple Procedure Rules to mention a remit to the summary cause roll preclude that course of action?

It is conceivable that a simple procedure claim could evolve into a dispute which could competently be resolved only on the summary cause roll. Assume that Keith claims to have purchased a white bicycle from a vendor who refuses to deliver it. He raises a simple procedure claim for delivery with an alternative claim for £1500. Another customer Ken asserts that he purchased the item and seeks to enter the case as an additional respondent. He does so by applying under 9.8. If the sheriff grants the application the case will become a multiplepoinding, which cannot be entertained in simple procedure and it would have to be transferred to the summary cause roll. If he does not grant the application, Ken could raise a summary cause multiplepoinding calling both Keith and the vendor as parties and the simple procedure claim would become redundant. Disposing of it would not be straightforward however, because Ken would have no right of audience in that. Of course, if Simple Procedure (Special Claims) Rules were promulgated, as was supposed to happen by 2018, this conundrum would not arise.

17.3 deals with a reference to the Court of Justice of the European Union. In over thirty-five years of appearing in thousands of cases in Glasgow Sheriff Court (during most of which time the U.K. was a EU member state) the author has moved for such a referral once, that was in an ordinary action and the sheriff reacted with bafflement and a nervous glance at the sheriff clerk as if to seek a lifeline. The author has never observed or heard of anyone else making such a motion. Form 17A is headed "CJEU Referral" Incidentally, the author once conducted a proof before the same sheriff, an ex-procurator fiscal, in which the pursuer was referred to as "the Crown".

17.4 and 17.5 concern interventions by the Equality and Human Rights Commission and the Scottish Commission for Human Rights. The former was established by the Equality Act 2006, which Act it is designed to enforce. Section 30(2) gives it the "capacity to ... intervene" specifically in Scotland. The latter was created by the Scottish Commission for Human Rights Act 2006. Section 14 gives it the "power to intervene" in civil proceedings. It can do so only with the leave of the court or at the invitation of the court. If one of these organisations wishes to intervene it must lodge a Form17B, Application to Intervene. If the sheriff wishes to ask one of them to intervene she must send to it a Form 17C, Invitation to Intervene.

In response to a Freedom of Information Request submitted by the author the E.H.R.C. advised that it had intervened in one sheriff court case and that "This was in relation to an adult with incapacity" (response dated 19th August 2024). In reply to a similar enquiry the S.C.H.R. advised (on 6th August 2024) that it "has never intervened in the sheriff court".

Anyone raising a simple procedure claim under section 114 of the Equality Act 2010 must send a copy to the E.H.R.C. Incidentally, great care needs to be taken over instructions to raise such an action due to the complicated time bar provisions. Section 118 provides for six and nine-month time periods or such other period as the "sheriff thinks just and equitable". It is critical to read that section carefully. Otherwise, one could be facing a negligence claim, never mind a complaint to the S.L.C.C.

Section 114 refers to the sheriff granting "an application to stay or sist proceedings", which will mean nothing to a party litigant accustomed to the term "pause" in the simple procedure rules.

Of far more practical importance, 17.6 to 17.10 concern "damages management orders" if a claimant under a legal disability asks for payment or money, or someone else asks for payment to that person. These orders are competent only where the entitled person is over 16. The sheriff may order payment to the Accountant of Court, sheriff clerk, guardian or the person himself. In terms of the Judicial Factors Act 1849 the Accountant of Court is the accountant of the Court of Session although her office is at Hadrian House, Falkirk, which is shared with the Office of the Public Guardian. It is unclear whether the term guardian means one appointed in terms of section 57 of the Adults with Incapacity (Scotland) Act 2000 only, or whether it includes a continuing attorney as governed by Section 15. It would be odd if the latter were excluded, although it would be easy for the Rule to include "continuing attorney"; it does not. The annotations to the Court of Session section of the *Parliament House Book* suggest that normally, a sum up to £5000 could appropriately be administered by parents. That seems sensible. Small awards – which means all simple procedure awards – should not be entangled in bureaucratic knots.

It is competent to apply to the sheriff court by means of an Application to Change a Damages Management Order; the relative form is Form 17D. The person seeking to have the terms of the order altered completes parts A, B and C and sends it to the sheriff clerk and the other party. Part C is the application portion of the form. The other party must complete part D (Response) and send it to the court within 10 days. Once the sheriff has these representations she can either grant the application, refuse it or put it out to call for a discussion.

There is a quite separate Form 17E, headed Application for Instructions About a Damages Management Order. This is for the use of a person seeking directions from the court as to how the funds must be managed. The procedure described immediately above in relation to Form 17D applies *mutatis mutandis* to Form 17E and indeed to Form17F (see below).

17.11 and 17.12 concern child's property administration orders. The risks here are obvious; giving a child a sum of money might lead to its being spent on computer games and designer trainers rather than being invested in a sensible portfolio. A parent entrusted with the cash might squander it on wine, women (or men) and song. The basis for child's property administration orders is section 13 of the Children (Scotland) Act 1995. However, that section states that in any action in which any sum is payable to a child the court may make such order as it sees fit and without prejudice to the generality of that it can appoint a judicial factor, the sheriff clerk, the Accountant of Court or the child's parent or guardian. "Child" is not defined in the Glossary to the Simple Procedure Rules but it is in section 13 of the Act; it means anyone under 16.

That Act, incidentally, defines "child" as someone under 16 for some purposes and someone under 18 for others. This means that a 17-year old applicant is treated as an adult for the purposes of the 1995 Act and indeed the Age of Legal Capacity (Scotland) Act 1991 but if she were to give evidence she would be regarded as a child for the purposes of the Vulnerable Witnesses (Scotland) Act 2004 and Rule 11.

In *S v Argyll and Clyde Acute Hospitals NHS Trust* [2009] CSOH 43 Lord Brodie stated that the purpose of S13 is to put the monies "into the hands of the person best placed to administer them for the benefit of the child". The damages in that case were over £5,000,000, but the principle applies to all levels of the civil courts. It is competent to apply to the sheriff court by means of an Application to Change a Child's Property Administration Order. This is Form 17F. There is no mechanism to apply for instructions about a child's property administration order. Accordingly, there is no form equivalent to Form 17E.

17.13 and 17.14 relate to Equality Act 2010 claims. Section 114 of the Act explains how a remedy may lie in relation to the provision of services, exercise of public functions etc. A useful case on quantifying a discrimination claim is *Purves v Joydisc Ltd 2003 SLT (Sh Ct) 64* in which the sheriff principal awarded £1000 when a guide dog was forbidden from entering premises.

17.15 empowers the sheriff to transfer a 2020 Act claim from simple procedure to the Employment Tribunal. That forum also uses the terms applicant and respondent, so there is no clash of names in such a transition. 17.16 concerns the reverse; where the Employment Tribunal transfers such a claim to simple procedure. 17.17 applies where a National Security issue arises in a 2020 Act Claim. Since this is a practical guide to simple procedure it is not proposed to devote further space to these rarities.

THE FUTURE OF SIMPLE PROCEDURE

Informality of the kind promoted by the Rules is a round peg in a square hole. The author's view is that small value claims should not be processed in the sheriff court. Instead, that forum should have a privative jurisdiction of at least £7000, (the 2024 equivalent of 2016's £5000), and jurisdiction over any claim worth less than that figure ought to be transferred to a Small Claim Tribunal, similar to the type that operates in New Zealand rather than the First Tier Tribunal which is still presided over by lawyers. Scottish courts are adversarial in character and always have been. It is in their nature. If small value claims are to be treated inquisitorially they need to be in a forum other than a court. The system needs to be far more assistive too in facilitating the enforcement of decrees, perhaps by having post-decree hearings to deal with recovery of the debt. That would take funding, and needs to be resourced adequately. This applies to the whole system. Civil Online should allow costs to be reduced.

Whether the Scottish Small Claim Tribunal happens or not, it is true that the Small Claims Rules have evolved in sensible ways so far. Good changes have included the introduction of a multipurpose Form 9A, a flowchart and the abolition of the need to lodge a witness list and inventory of productions at the Claim Form and Response Form lodging stage. One hopes that this process of improvement will continue. In the meantime, solicitors need to be mindful of the risks highlighted in this book.

MORE BOOKS BY LAW BRIEF PUBLISHING

A selection of our other titles available now:-

'A Practical Guide to Probation Breaches and Other Applications' by Mark Thomas
'A Practical Guide to Remarriage and Divorce' by Cordelia Williams & Claire Howard
'A Practical Guide to Privacy, Transparency, Reporting Restrictions and Closed Proceedings in the Court of Protection' by Laura Mannering
'Beaumont on Barristers – A Guide to Defending Disciplinary Proceedings (Second Edition)' by Marc Beaumont
'A Practical Guide to Payments for Environmental Services' by Ben Sharples
'A Practical Guide to the Law of Pregnancy and Maternity at Work' by Rebecca Thomas
'A Practical Guide to Redundancy – Second Edition' by Philip Hyland & Collette Moore
'A Practical Guide to International Issues for Scottish Family Lawyers' by Susie Mountain, Donna McKay, Ken MacDonald
'A Practical Guide to the Law on Deprivation of Liberty' by Ben Troke
'A Practical Guide to Rights over Airspace and Subsoil – Second Edition' by Daniel Gatty
'A Practical Guide to the Law in Relation to Inquests' by Ramya Nagesh
'A Practical Guide to the Construction and Rectification of Wills and Trust Instruments (Second Edition)' by Edward Hewitt
'A Practical Guide to Data Protection in Social Housing' by Clare Paterson
'A Practical Guide to Spousal Maintenance – Second Edition' by Liz Cowell
'A Practical Guide to International Parental Child Abduction Law (England and Wales)' by Dr Onyója Momoh
'A Practical Guide to Deprivation of British Citizenship' by Sean Ell
'A Practical Guide to Commercial Property Service Charges' by Rachel Garton
'A Practical Guide to Clinical Negligence – Third Edition' by Geoffrey Simpson-Scott (Geoff)
'A Practical Guide to the Rights of Grandparents in Children Proceedings – Second Edition' by Stuart Barlow

'The Electronic Communications Code: A Practical Guide – Second Edition' by Kerry Bretherton KC, James Castle, Mark Loveday
'A Practical Guide to the Independent School Standards – September 2023 Edition' by Sarah McKimm
'A Practical Guide to Estate Administration and Crypto Assets' by Richard Marshall
'A Practical Guide to Parental Alienation in Private and Public Law Children Cases' by Sam King QC & Frankie Shama
'Contested Heritage – Removing Art from Land and Historic Buildings' by Richard Harwood QC, Catherine Dobson, David Sawtell
'The Limits of Separate Legal Personality: When Those Running a Company Can Be Held Personally Liable for Losses Caused to Third Parties Outside of the Company' by Dr Mike Wilkinson
'A Practical Guide to Transgender Law' by Robin Moira White & Nicola Newbegin
'A Practical Guide to 'Stranded Spouses' in Family Law' by Mani Singh Basi
'A Practical Guide to Residential Freehold Conveyancing' by Lorraine Richardson
'A Practical Guide to Pensions on Divorce for Lawyers' by Bryan Scant
'A Practical Guide to Challenging Sham Marriage Allegations in Immigration Law' by Priya Solanki
'A Practical Guide to Digital Communications Evidence in Criminal Law' by Sam Willis
'A Practical Guide to Legal Rights in Scotland' by Sarah-Jane Macdonald
'A Practical Guide to New Build Conveyancing' by Paul Sams & Rebecca East
'A Practical Guide to Inherited Wealth on Divorce' by Hayley Trim
'A Practical Guide to Practice Direction 12J and Domestic Abuse in Private Law Children Proceedings' by Rebecca Cross & Malvika Jaganmohan
'A Practical Guide to Confiscation and Restraint' by Narita Bahra QC, John Carl Townsend, David Winch
'A Practical Guide to the Law of Forests in Scotland' by Philip Buchan
'A Practical Guide to Health and Medical Cases in Immigration Law' by Rebecca Chapman & Miranda Butler
'A Practical Guide to Bad Character Evidence for Criminal Practitioners by Aparna Rao
'A Practical Guide to Extradition Law post-Brexit' by Myles Grandison et al
'A Practical Guide to Hoarding and Mental Health for Housing Lawyers' by Rachel Coyle

'Stephens on Contractual Indemnities' by Richard Stephens

'A Practical Guide to the EU Succession Regulation' by Richard Frimston

'A Practical Guide to Solicitor and Client Costs – Second Edition' by Robin Dunne

'Constructive Dismissal – Practice Pointers and Principles' by Benjimin Burgher

'A Practical Guide to Religion and Belief Discrimination Claims in the Workplace' by Kashif Ali

'A Practical Guide to the Law of Medical Treatment Decisions' by Ben Troke

'Fundamental Dishonesty and QOCS in Personal Injury Proceedings: Law and Practice' by Jake Rowley

'A Practical Guide to the Law in Relation to School Exclusions' by Charlotte Hadfield & Alice de Coverley

'A Practical Guide to Divorce for the Silver Separators' by Karin Walker

'The Right to be Forgotten – The Law and Practical Issues' by Melissa Stock

'A Practical Guide to Planning Law and Rights of Way in National Parks, the Broads and AONBs' by James Maurici QC, James Neill et al

'A Practical Guide to Election Law' by Tom Tabori

'A Practical Guide to the Law in Relation to Surrogacy' by Andrew Powell

'A Practical Guide to Claims Arising from Fatal Accidents – Second Edition' by James Patience

'A Practical Guide to Asbestos Claims' by Jonathan Owen & Gareth McAloon

'A Practical Guide to Stamp Duty Land Tax in England and Northern Ireland' by Suzanne O'Hara

'A Practical Guide to the Law of Farming Partnerships' by Philip Whitcomb

'A Practical Guide to the Law of Unlawful Eviction and Harassment – Second Edition' by Stephanie Lovegrove

'A Practical Guide to Costs in Personal Injury Claims – Second Edition' by Matthew Hoe

'A Practical Guide to the General Data Protection Regulation (GDPR) – Second Edition' by Keith Markham

'A Practical Guide to Working with Litigants in Person and McKenzie Friends in Family Cases' by Stuart Barlow

'Protecting Unregistered Brands: A Practical Guide to the Law of Passing Off' by Lorna Brazell

'A Practical Guide to Secondary Liability and Joint Enterprise Post-Jogee' by Joanne Cecil & James Mehigan

'A Practical Guide to the Pre-Action RTA Claims Protocol for Personal Injury Lawyers' by Antonia Ford
'A Practical Guide to Neighbour Disputes and the Law' by Alexander Walsh
'A Practical Guide to Coercive Control for Legal Practitioners and Victims' by Rachel Horman
'A Practical Guide to the Law of Driverless Cars – Second Edition'
by Alex Glassbrook, Emma Northey & Scarlett Milligan
'A Practical Guide to TOLATA Claims' by Greg Williams
'A Practical Guide to Elderly Law – Second Edition' by Justin Patten
'A Practical Guide to Responding to Housing Disrepair and Unfitness Claims' by Iain Wightwick
'A Practical Guide to the Law of Bullying and Harassment in the Workplace' by Philip Hyland
'How to Be a Freelance Solicitor: A Practical Guide to the SRA-Regulated Freelance Solicitor Model' by Paul Bennett
'A Practical Guide to Prison Injury Claims' by Malcolm Johnson
'A Practical Guide to Advising Clients at the Police Station' by Colin Stephen McKeown-Beaumont
'A Practical Guide to Antisocial Behaviour Injunctions – Second Edition' by Iain Wightwick
'Practical Mediation: A Guide for Mediators, Advocates, Advisers, Lawyers, and Students in Civil, Commercial, Business, Property, Workplace, and Employment Cases' by Jonathan Dingle with John Sephton
'The Mini-Pupillage Workbook' by David Boyle
'A Practical Guide to Crofting Law' by Brian Inkster
'A Practical Guide to the Law of Domain Names and Cybersquatting' by Andrew Clemson
'A Practical Guide to the Law of Gender Pay Gap Reporting' by Harini Iyengar
'NHS Whistleblowing and the Law' by Joseph England
'Employment Law and the Gig Economy' by Nigel Mackay & Annie Powell
'A Practical Guide to Noise Induced Hearing Loss (NIHL) Claims' by Andrew Mckie, Ian Skeate, Gareth McAloon
'An Introduction to Beauty Negligence Claims – A Practical Guide for the Personal Injury Practitioner' by Greg Almond
'Intercompany Agreements for Transfer Pricing Compliance' by Paul Sutton
'Zen and the Art of Mediation' by Martin Plowman
'A Practical Guide to Adoption for Family Lawyers' by Graham Pegg

'A Practical Guide to Industrial Disease Claims' by Andrew Mckie & Ian Skeate
'A Practical Guide to Conducting a Sheriff Court Proof' by Andrew Stevenson
'A Practical Guide to Vicarious Liability' by Mariel Irvine
'A Practical Guide to Applications for Landlord's Consent and Variation of Leases' by Mark Shelton
'A Practical Guide to Relief from Sanctions Post-Mitchell and Denton' by Peter Causton
'A Practical Guide to Equity Release for Advisors' by Paul Sams
'A Practical Guide to Financial Services Claims' by Chris Hegarty
'A Practical Guide to Financial Ombudsman Service Claims' by Adam Temple & Robert Scrivenor
'A Practical Guide to Running Housing Disrepair and Cavity Wall Claims – Second Edition' by Andrew Mckie & Ian Skeate
'A Practical Guide to Holiday Sickness Claims – Second Edition' by Andrew Mckie & Ian Skeate
'Arguments and Tactics for Personal Injury and Clinical Negligence Claims' by Dorian Williams
'A Practical Guide to Drone Law' by Rufus Ballaster, Andrew Firman, Eleanor Clot
'On Experts: CPR35 for Lawyers and Experts' by David Boyle
'An Introduction to Personal Injury Law' by David Boyle

These books and more are available to order online direct from the publisher at www.lawbriefpublishing.com, where you can also read free sample chapters. For any queries, call us on 0844 587 2383 or email us at mail@lawbriefpublishing.com.

Our books are all generally in stock at www.amazon.co.uk with free next day delivery for Prime members, and at good legal bookshops such as Wildy & Sons.

We are regularly launching new books in our series of practical day-to-day practitioners' guides. Visit our website and join our free newsletter to be kept informed and to receive special offers, free chapters, etc.

You can also follow us on Twitter at www.twitter.com/lawbriefpub.

www.ingramcontent.com/pod-product-compliance
Lightning Source LLC
LaVergne TN
LVHW052324200926
848481LV00002B/663